Introduction to Traditional Natal Astrology:

A Complete Working Guide for Modern Astrologers

Charles Obert

Almuten Press

Minneapolis, Minnesota

2015

Published and printed in the United States of America

By Almuten Press

3507 Taylor Street NE, Minneapolis, MN 55418

©2015 by Charles Obert

ISBN-13: 978-0-9864187-0-9

This book is dedicated to

Dr. Benjamin N. Dykes, Ph. D.

Astrologer, Scholar, Translator,

Teacher and Friend

Acknowledgements

Very special thanks go to my astrologer friend Beth Krause, who worked very hard with me through multiple drafts of this book, giving me valuable feedback, criticism and encouragement. This book is far stronger thanks to all her work, and I am grateful.

I also want to thank my other astrologer friends, Tony VanArx, Maddie Youngstrom, and Shawn Nygaard, who read the book in manuscript form and gave valuable feedback.

And finally, my general thanks to the members of the Traditional Astrology Study Group here in Minneapolis, Minnesota. That group served as the school and laboratory in which the interpretation rules of this book were worked out, tested and refined.

Chart illustrations and tables came from several astrology programs, including Solar Fire Gold, Janus, and Sirius.

Contents

Section Six: Examples of Interpretation

Section Seven: Concluding Material

Index of Figures

Index of Tables

"The whole divine economy is pervaded by Providence. Even the vagaries of chance have their place in Nature's scheme; that is, in the intricate tapestry of the ordinances of Providence. Providence is the source from which all things flow; and allied with it is Necessity, and the welfare of the universe. You yourself are a part of that universe; and for any one of nature's parts, that which is assigned to it by the World-Nature or helps to keep it in being are good."

- Marcus Aurelius, **Meditations**

Part One:

Concepts and Elements

of

Traditional Astrology

Section One:
Introduction and Worldview

Chapter One:
General Introduction

The purpose of this book is to provide a usable and structured framework for the study and practice of traditional Western natal astrology. It is intended to be an introduction to the viewpoint and techniques of traditional astrology.

This book concentrates on a usable set of core techniques that can be used as a framework for further work and study.

What is traditional astrology?

Traditional astrology refers to the art of astrology as it was practiced in the West from the Hellenistic era, beginning around the second century BC, up through the early Renaissance, which was the era of the last of the famous English astrologers, like William Lilly, John Gadbury, and Nicolas Culpeper.

While there are definite differences in technique and emphasis within that time frame, there is also a large, strong and recognizable body of shared techniques and meanings. After that period astrology went into decline, and when it experienced a revival in the late 19th century (with people like Alan Leo), many of the details of the tradition had been lost.

Audience

This book is intended for people who already have some familiarity with the basics of astrology. It is not intended as a stand-alone beginner's text.

It is primarily intended for modern astrologers who are interested in learning techniques of traditional astrology, whether to practice them exclusively or to use them to complement their modern techniques.

If you are completely new to astrology, you will want to supplement this book with a good comprehensive modern text. I list some good books to consider in the Suggested Reading list at the end of the book, including a good short beginner's text.

I am not assuming that people using this book will want to drop modern astrology altogether and practice only traditional techniques. This book can be useful and interesting to modern astrologers who want to learn traditional techniques, perhaps incorporate some of them into their work, or use these techniques to provide an alternate point of view. That is how I personally use both traditional and modern astrology, as two different approaches that give me complementary meanings.

Natal

This book concentrates solely on the subject of traditional natal astrology. Most of the material currently available by living authors on traditional astrology concentrates on horary, and not all of that translates into natal interpretation.

Practical

This book is not meant to be primarily academic or scholarly. I am writing for people who wish to practice traditional natal interpretation. I do not include anything in this book that I have not tested and found useful in my own experience.

Much of the content of this book comes out of a study group on Traditional Natal Astrology that I facilitated in Minneapolis, Minnesota since 2012. The participants included Dr. Benjamin Dykes, who is a scholar and translator of medieval astrology works, and Estelle Daniels, who has been studying and practicing traditional astrology for many years, including the period when very few source texts were available. Their scholarship and experience has been invaluable, and I have learned a lot from both of them.

During that same period I was a student of Hellenistic astrologer Chris Brennan's excellent online course, which also influenced the content of this book. Information on Chris and his website is in the Suggested Reading list.

Main Book Sections

There are two main parts to this book.

In the first part, I lay out the worldview and elements of traditional astrology. This is to provide the basic framework and vocabulary of techniques.

In the second part, which I consider to be the heart of the book, I present a basic outline for doing natal chart interpretation. This is followed by a series of fully worked out examples of natal chart interpretation using traditional astrology techniques.

So, I will present the tools, and present many examples of using them in context. Hopefully this will give you what you need to work with traditional astrology techniques in your own chart interpretation.

What is Not Covered

This book is not exhaustive, and there are important elements of traditional astrology that will not be covered. They include the following.

First, the fixed stars were considered important. My sense is that they were most important in the context of mundane astrology, and were not as significant within natal work.

Temperament is related to the four elements, and is a way of determining basic character or disposition. While this does add detail to a chart interpretation, it is not an essential element.

There are numerous detailed descriptions of how aspects either perfected or were prevented from perfecting, including translation of light, collection of light, refranation and so on. These are important in the context of horary astrology, but not as significant for natal.

A Personal Note

I want to take a minute to talk a little bit about the reasons that I wrote this book.

First of all, when I first started seriously studying traditional astrology some years ago, I felt overwhelmed by what seemed like the sheer amount of material that needed to be covered. It was very hard to approach. There were enormous amounts of detail without any clear organizing principles, and I felt like I needed to circle over the texts, over and over, until I got a sense of the pattern and order that pervaded the system.

Also, the bulk of the modern material available on traditional astrology concentrates on horary, I think largely because this was the main focus of William Lilly, whose book, *Christian Astrology*, is easily the most influential book on traditional astrology in the English language. The third book of Lilly's masterwork does cover natal astrology, but it seems that little has been done to follow up on that. It was reading the third volume of *Christian Astrology* that first gave me the idea to do this book several years ago.

So this book presents a synthesis of the main concepts of traditional astrology as applied to natal chart reading, with a tip of the hat to William Lilly, *Christian Astrology* book three.

That was the first purpose.

As I got further into this project, I was increasingly struck by how much of traditional astrology is presented as *over against* modern astrology. The astrology community seemed divided into two camps on this topic; you practiced either traditional or modern, and neither side seemed to have much sympathy and understanding for the other.

I don't want to perpetuate that division.

I am trying to present traditional astrology in a way that does stand in contrast to much modern astrology, but I have tried to do it in a way that does justice to the strengths and weaknesses of each. I am now convinced that traditional and modern astrology have complementary strengths and weaknesses and have a lot to learn from each other. I want to be part of the process of getting a dialog going.

So, summing up, this book has two purposes.

- First, to present traditional astrology in an organized, approachable and workable way. By the time you are done with this book I want you to be able to take a natal chart and the interpretation outline and be able to work through it, and see how the traditional astrology techniques work out in practice. I also want you to be able to go back to the original texts and have a workable conceptual context to read and study them with benefit.

- And second, to present traditional astrology in such a way that it complements modern astrology rather than being opposed to it. Each has their own strengths and weaknesses, and I want to present them in a fair and balanced way. I want to act as a bridge builder between the two communities.

If I have succeeded in a small way in either of those points, then this book has accomplished its intended purpose.

Chapter Two:
How is traditional Western astrology different from modern?

Introduction

In traditional and modern astrology as practiced today there seems to be a common perception that the two systems are in some way opposed or separate, and you need to practice either one or the other.

Unfortunately, I have often seen writing in which practicing traditional astrologers have felt the need to criticize or cut down modern astrology - and, of course, many modern astrologers have returned the favor. I have seen this in published books and articles, and far too often in discussions and chat groups on the Internet. Very often, I find that those who attack the other school are setting up paper dragons and cutting down positions that are not actually held by the practitioners of the other style.

In conversation and shared meetings, I see significant differences in how I read from the tools and perspective of most modern astrologers I know. While there is a strong core of shared meaning, I also see a lot of significant differences in techniques used. Also, there seems to be distinct differences in the overall philosophy and point of view with which we each approach reading charts.

So, along with covering techniques, I will also talk about overall differences in philosophy and viewpoint between traditional and modern astrology.

I hope that you will see that there is a great deal of overlap between traditional astrology and good modern techniques; modern astrologers do not need to start over in order to work with the material in this book. There are many modern astrologers writing and practicing today whose writings and work I admire and learn from.

However, I also think there will be areas that modern astrologers approaching traditional astrology for the first time will want to question or at least temporarily suspend some of the common assumptions that they use, in order to really comprehend and use this traditional material.

The Differences

Modern astrology is more psychological and character-oriented; traditional is more external, situational and event oriented.

In modern astrology the chart is primarily a map of your mind; in traditional astrology it is primarily your external circumstances and what happens to you.

This is a major *shift in perspective*.

Take an example of a native with Mars in the 7th house of relationships.

In traditional astrology that Mars would describe the kinds of partners that person has. The interpretation is not in the person's character but in their outer world, the actual people - partners and enemies - who fall under the subject of the 7th house.

A modern astrologer, used to the chart being all inside your mind, would say this means you are 'projecting' the Mars and not 'owning' it. A modern astrologer typically starts with how that Mars describes the native; a traditional astrologer starts with how that Mars describes 7th house people and circumstances.

The traditional approach is not a matter of a person projecting a part of themselves onto someone else; this is a different model. The context of a natal chart in modern is the person's character. In traditional, it is the person within the larger context of their external circumstances.

I think this is one of the major differences in perspective between traditional and modern.

There is an important implication of this change in perspective. In modern astrology you would speak of using the chart to look for ways the person can harmonize different parts of themselves. In traditional astrology, you are looking for ways to *harmonize how a person fits within a larger external context*.

Does this mean that your interpretation needs to be either character analysis or external event and situation based? No. I think *both* work, and are equally valuable. Traditional does emphasize the external situations, people and events much more strongly than modern. I think this is a place that modern astrology can recover more of the external meaning of the chart, while traditional astrology can benefit by integrating more of the character analysis of modern astrology.

And, I think this can help astrology recover a perspective that assumes an *ongoing connectedness to, and harmony within, a larger external world order*.

Please note that this does *not* mean that traditional astrology is only trying to predict specific events. It is more accurate to say that it describes classes or types of events. Using our earlier example of Mars in the 7th house, this would mean partners or adversaries that display Martial characteristics, and that can manifest in a wide variety of ways.

Fate and Free Will

Much of modern astrology subscribes to a kind of open-ended, indeterminate free will – in other words, your natal chart may show certain tendencies, but they can all be changed or 'transcended' with hard work, and often with positive thinking. In modern astrology in my experience, a heavy emphasis is put on interpreting the chart only in positive terms.

Traditional astrology is rooted in a worldview that is more deterministic or fate-based. Another way of putting it is that traditional astrology operates in a larger context than the individual human psyche. In traditional astrology you are not so much looking to 'transcend' your chart as to understand or divine (divination, learning the will of the divine) your place in the overall order. I think of it as aligning yourself with the order of the universe and how you happen to fit in it. In that way it is similar to divination systems like I Ching.

While modern astrology de-emphasizes fate and emphasizes free will, older traditional astrology texts strongly emphasize fate, and minimize free will and choice. Just as modern astrology texts often dwell exclusively on positive use of the planets, many traditional texts are very dualistic and have extremes of good and evil outcomes, so they can come across as fatalistic and judgmental.

I think that human experience includes both dimensions, fate and free will, and our astrology needs to include both. Sometimes emphasizing how a person can make best use of a situation is appropriate, and sometimes it is appropriate to accept that there are external events out of our control for which no-one is to blame. As in much of our experience, a balance of the two perspectives seems to be most fruitful and most realistic.

Evaluating Planetary Condition

Modern astrology has largely lost the sense of planets being positive or negative, fortunately or unfortunately placed. It tends to view all charts as equally fortunate, all people having an equal chance for a successful life in the usual terms. Where there are challenges in charts, much modern astrology emphasizes taking a positive approach to them.

Traditional astrology places a heavy emphasis on evaluating the condition of planets, sometimes fortunate and sometimes very unfortunate. Also, some planets are naturally helpful or benefic, and some are naturally disruptive or malefic. In traditional astrology all charts are not created equal, and not all planets are equally effective; some people are, if you will, fated for success, or good marriages, or wealth, and some are fated to have rough lives in different ways.

So traditional astrology is much more focused towards a realistic evaluation of a chart and how it works out in your life, rather than a psychological description of your psychological potential. Traditional astrology does not ignore or gloss over difficult or negative aspects of the chart, nor does it emphasize only being positive. Also, to be fair, traditional astrology can sometimes be severe, and needs to be used with compassion. Like in Reinhold Niebuhr's serenity prayer, we pray for the wisdom to discern between those things we can change, and those things we must only accept.

Differences in Technique and Emphasis

Traditional astrology does not emphasize signs as strongly as modern, and emphasizes planets much more than modern. In traditional astrology, signs do not act - they provide an environment that conditions the quality of the planets in them.

Rather than being major personality types, signs in traditional astrology are used mostly as environments within which the various planets can function, sometimes effectively, sometimes ineffectively. The most important facts about the sign are, where is the ruler of that sign and what shape is it in (in traditional astrology language, what is its dignity or debility), and what other planets are in that sign and what shape are they in.

Traditional astrology does not use the modern Twelve Letter Alphabet, in which the houses, signs and planets correspond.

Much of modern astrology assumes that the 12 houses correspond in meaning to the 12 Zodiac signs. In modern astrology the first sign, Aries, corresponds in meaning to the first house, and the first house is also related to Mars, the ruler of Aries. The first, fifth and ninth houses are called the fire houses because they correspond to the 3 fire signs, Aries, Leo and Sagittarius.

This correspondence in modern astrology is widely assumed and ubiquitous.

In modern astrology texts that cover meaning of the planets, it is very common to see a section on the meaning of the planet in Aries or in the first house, Taurus or the second house, and so on, which assumes that signs and houses correspond in meaning.

Zipporah Dobyns codified this as what she called the 12 Letter Alphabet, and in her widely influential system, Sign equals Planet equals House. While not all modern astrology pushes the correspondence to the point of equation as in her system, the correspondence in meaning between houses, signs, and their ruling planets, is pretty much universally assumed.

This is very much a late 20th century innovation and does not appear at all widely prior to that.

Historically it is likely that the meanings of the houses and the meanings of the signs developed separately, possibly from two different civilizations, and there is little or nothing in traditional texts to indicate any equation in meaning of the two.

So, traditional astrology does not associate the ruler of the first sign Aries with the first house, Venus with the second house and so on. There is no necessary connection between the Moon and the 4th house, or the Sun and the 5th. Having Venus in the 2nd house does not have any necessary similarity with having Venus in Taurus.

I think that saying that signs and houses correspond is an oversimplification. I also think that saying they do not correspond is an oversimplification in the other direction. Like many things in astrology, the truth is more complex, and lies somewhere in the middle.

While I think there are some general parallels in meaning between the sequence of signs and the houses, I think that some important dimensions of their individual meaning are lost by assuming their correspondence. In this work, since I am covering traditional astrology, I will deal with them separately.

Traditional astrology has an emphasis on sect as defining the overall strength and weakness of the planets.

There are two sects in traditional astrology, day and night, also called diurnal and nocturnal. Charts are either diurnal or nocturnal depending on whether the Sun is above or below the horizon. The different planets are either diurnal or nocturnal also, and the quality of their function is greatly influenced whether they agree or disagree with the sect of the chart. Sect will be covered in detail in a later section, and you will see that is a major element in chart interpretation.

Whole sign aspects, seeing and aversion.

The form of traditional astrology I practice uses Whole Sign houses, which go back to the Hellenistic era and were used for over a millennium. In Whole Sign houses all of the sign the Ascendant is in is the first house, all of the next sign is the second, so sign and house boundaries coincide.

In traditional astrology, the inter-relations or aspects between planets are based on the metaphor of sight. Planets in aspect can see each other; planets not in aspect are out of sight or in aversion, which means turned away, and there is a lack of communication.

In traditional astrology, a planet anywhere in Cancer is trine a planet anywhere in Pisces, regardless of how close they are by degree.

Traditional astrology also uses degree-based aspects, but for different purposes.

Traditional astrology uses only what are called the Ptolemaic aspects – sextile, square, trine, and opposition. (Conjunctions are also used, but strictly speaking they are not aspects.) A planet that aspects another planet can 'see' that planet. Planets that do not have one of these aspects are considered to be averse and cannot see each other, so there is a lack of awareness and communication between them.

The meaning and use of aspects in traditional is quite different in some ways from the modern use. This will be discussed in detail in the chapter on aspects. I personally use both traditional and modern ways of viewing aspects, but I find that they have different shades of meaning and complement each other.

Rulership or Dignity is much more heavily emphasized and used.

There are multiple levels of rulers used – lord or ruler, exaltation, trigon or triplicity, bound or term, and face, and all but face seem to have been widely used. Modern astrology uses only ruler and exaltation, and they are not emphasized. Also, rulership in general, and reception as showing relationship between planets, are much more strongly emphasized in traditional than modern.

In the basic framework that I present here, I will concentrate on the two most important dignities of rulership and exaltation. I personally use the minor dignity of bound or term mostly in predictive work, which is beyond the scope of this book.

So, with its focus on rulership and dignity, traditional astrology pays much more attention to evaluating the condition of planets for interpretation.

For instance, a modern astrologer looking at Mars in Libra might say something about how the person tries to express assertion in a peaceful way. A traditional astrologer starts by noting that Mars is in its detriment in Libra, and thus is likely to act in an erratic or unbalanced way. This would be further modified by the location and condition of Venus, the ruler of Libra, and what condition that planet was in. It is a more nuanced way to judge the probable *quality* of a planet's action.

Traditional astrology uses only traditional rulerships.

Whether or not you use the outer planets with traditional astrology, Mars rules Scorpio, Jupiter rules Pisces, Saturn rules Aquarius.

Different meaning of rulership

In traditional astrology, rulership does not mean affinity; it means that the planet is in charge of the affairs of that sign. For example, if Taurus is on the cusp of your seventh house, the location and condition of Venus are going to largely determine the nature and quality of your relationships.

Some traditional astrologers use the 3 modern planets, some do not.

In practice, almost all the traditional astrologers I know, including myself, do include Uranus, Neptune and Pluto when reading. However, in general, those traditional astrologers who do use the outer planets do not emphasize them anywhere nearly as strongly as many modern astrologers do.

In my own practice, when I look at a chart I first do a core reading with only the Sacred Seven traditional planets, and only add in the three modern planets after I have established a basic framework of interpretation.

Chapter Three:
History and Philosophy

Definition of Western Astrology

Western astrology has its roots in Egypt and Babylonia, and first came together as the grand synthesis we recognize as our astrology system during the Hellenistic era. This is the age when first Greece and then Rome dominated the Mediterranean in what we call the Western world. This is the root of the culture that then came to dominate Europe and North America.

The other main branch of astrology that has connections with ours is what we in the West call Vedic or Indian astrology, and what is referred to as Jyotish by its practitioners. That is also sometimes called Eastern astrology as opposed to our Western system.

At the height of the Hellenistic era there was communication and trade between the Mediterranean civilization and India, and there was a definite cross-fertilization of ideas and techniques. Vedic astrology has an unbroken tradition going back thousands of years, while here in the west we have lost much of our connection with our Hellenistic roots. For that reason, Hellenistic and Vedic astrology share some common characteristics that are not found in modern Western astrology.

Main Phases

The grand flowering of Hellenistic astrology was from roughly 1st century BC to 6th century AD.

After the fall of Rome and the ascendancy of the Christian empire in the West, astrology went out of style in the Christian countries. At that time, much of Western Hellenistic astrology was kept alive and developed in the Persian and later Arabic empires. This Persian and Arabic period continues to roughly the 10th century AD.

The Medieval era of astrology in the West began in the 1100's, when Arabic astrology texts were translated into Latin and introduced into Europe. This is also an era when Greek writers like Plato and Aristotle were being re-introduced to the West, and the period when what we call

Kabbalah was introduced.

The line of traditional astrology continued through the early Renaissance era, roughly the 1400's through 1600's. This is the time period of the last great traditional astrologers in the English language, including the astrology authors, William Lilly, John Gadbury, William Ramesey, and Nicholas Culpeper.

During this whole period of well over a thousand years, from the birth of Western astrology in the Hellenistic era up through the early Renaissance, there is a definite continuity to the tradition. There was some change and development, but there is also a coherency of outlook and technique through that period.

The Renaissance was also a period of a major transition in worldview. This became the modern scientific worldview, with a detached, value free model of the objective material universe. In that world model astrology no longer really made any coherent sense.

With the rise of the scientific worldview in the later Renaissance and afterwards there was a decline in the knowledge and practice of astrology. During this period there was a break in the transmission of the full tradition, and many techniques were lost.

The Re-Invention of Astrology

The revival of astrology in the 20th century was in some ways a new invention. Much of 20th century astrology was created partly to mirror the change in our world, and partly because enough of traditional Western astrology technique was lost that there was need for new techniques in order to have a functioning system.

As with many other areas in our world today, much of modern astrology has lost its sense of reverence for past tradition and of continuity with that tradition. New systems and techniques have been created, and astrology has been combined with concepts and techniques from other systems like psychology, Theosophy, and Hindu philosophy.

Revival of Traditional Astrology

For the last few decades there has been a wave of recovery and translation of older Western astrology texts. There has also been work to recover and use techniques from traditional astrology that had been lost.

This is not a merely theoretical exploration; researchers are finding that many of the traditional techniques work very well, and add another dimension of meaning to chart reading.

This period of recovery began with the rediscovery and reprinting of William Lilly's classic, *Christian Astrology*. Lilly practiced primarily horary astrology, so much of the modern material available on traditional astrology techniques is centered on Horary.

There are many noteworthy modern astrologers who have been working to recover traditional techniques. There are more than I can cover here, but I would like to mention a few of the most important who have influenced my own astrology and this book.

Lee Lehman practices what she calls classical astrology. She was one of the first modern astrologers to do comprehensive work with the multiple levels of dignity or rulership. The modern astrologer Kevin Burk has an introductory modern text that incorporates some of Lehman's work with dignities and is an interesting first fusion of traditional and modern.

Since the 1990's there has been the work of Project Hindsight, which was primarily a series of translations from the original Hellenistic texts. Project Hindsight includes Robert Hand, Robert Schmidt, and Robert Zoller. Unfortunately, almost of the translation series is out of print and unavailable.

Joseph Crane has published important work based on the Project Hindsight material.

Important translations of traditional texts have been done by James Holden, who died in 2014. More recently, the modern scholar of medieval astrology, Dr. Benjamin Dykes, has been doing an extensive series of translations from Latin, and very recently from Arabic. Both Chris Brennan and Demetra George have been doing important work in Hellenistic astrology, Deborah Houlding is doing outstanding work with the meaning of the houses and with horary astrology, and Christopher Warnock works in Renaissance astrology.

I am hoping the 21st century continues a trend of integrating the best of traditional astrology techniques in with the best of 20th century astrology that seems to be standing the test of time. I am hoping that this book helps to open the door to traditional astrology techniques for more new astrologers.

Philosophical Background

Along with learning the techniques, many people exploring traditional astrology are also interested in learning about and recovering the philosophical and spiritual worldviews that were current during the first flourishing of astrology in the civilization of Greece and Rome. The traditional techniques, and much of the meaning of astrology itself, take on more meaning when that context is understood.

Hellenistic astrology came together during the same period as the flowering of the greatest of the Greek philosophers, including Pythagoras, Aristotle, Plato, the Stoics, and the later Neo-Platonist School. There are a few main strands or components of this worldview that I would like to explore here.

First, it is very important to realize that the mythic world of the Greek, and later Roman, gods was still very much alive, and the gods were an assumed part of their thought and religious life. When considering different doctrines of their philosophy, it is important to keep that living mythic backdrop in mind. This is not a vague or abstract conceptual world; this is a living, breathing, interacting, tumultuous family of spiritual intelligences who played an important place in how the order of life on earth was played out.

Next there is Pythagoras, whose school and teachings had a strong influence on all following Greek philosophy. This is where we get the sort of mathematical mysticism that underlies astrology. The order of mathematics and geometry were considered to be important ways to apprehend the divinely ordained order of the cosmos.

In later Greek philosophy there were two main approaches to explaining how astrology could work, and why there was a correspondence between planetary positions and event in human life on earth.

On the one hand, Aristotle, and later Ptolemy, explained this as a direct causal influence of the planets on human behavior.

On the other hand, the Stoics taught that the planets signified or communicated meaning rather than being causal agents. The position and pattern of the planets could signify the will of the Divine in the world order. In that sense you could say that astrology communicated the will of the Gods to humanity.

With either perspective, astrology was an expression of a living and coherent universe, where humanity and earthly society had their ordained place in the overall divinely ordered pattern of the cosmos.

This worldview is very much fate-based, much more so than we can imagine in our modern world which assumes a high level of free will in action.

Later Development

In the Islamic and Christian era, there needed to be a change in approach to astrology to deal with an all-powerful God who both controlled all things in Heaven and earth, and allowed humans free-will to choose either for or against God.

Outside of the action of divine Grace, and the ability to choose for or against God, the human was controlled by the forces dealt with in astrology. Through grace, the human could transcend the workings of the planets. The planets and forces of astrology were then viewed as something like subsidiary beings like archangels or angels, acting under Divine control and Providence, and all things were ultimately subject to the Will of God. In that era, astrology was viewed as a way to learn God's will in a given matter, and was approached seriously and prayerfully, with much thought and meditative preparation.

We still have the remnants of this attitude in the modern belief that the planets control those who are not self-aware, but can be transcended with awareness and spiritual work. That is a modern version of the medieval Christian model of the human transcending the world through the grace of God; it is a very Christian sort of attitude.

Summing Up

The whole period of traditional Western astrology assumed a stable and ordered model of the Universe. The forces of astrology, the planets or gods, were very much alive and well at the peak of Hellenistic astrology, and stayed alive, though in a subsidiary position, during the Islamic and then Christian periods in the West.

It was not until the Renaissance, and the birth of what we now think of as the modern scientific worldview, that astrology went into decline because it had no coherent place in the newly emerging worldview.

The worldview of traditional astrology was coherent and alive, and was at once Mythical, Ordered by Reason, Mathematical and Geometrical.

The Cosmos was very much alive, and was ordered in a way that could be apprehended by human intelligence. Mathematics and geometry was a major part of that order. The aliveness of the planetary gods was an important assumed part of the order.

So astrology could be viewed in a couple of different ways.

1) It was a way of apprehending the divine order of the cosmos.

2) It was a way of ascertaining the will of God, or the will of the Gods, for human society.

3) And finally, it was a way that God and/or the Gods could communicate with humans.

There was no split into subjective and objective reality, or into a detached eternal scientific reality devoid of meaning, and an internal subjective meaningful order.

There was also no sense of the human existing separately from the order of society or of the cosmos; human life was contained within a larger context, and the whole notion of a human somehow having their own private reality or being separated from an external order was just not thinkable. The whole notion of an astrology that was just internal or focused on character analysis was unthinkable, since the notion of a person having an important existence outside of the larger societal and cosmic order just didn't exist.

The order of society and the order of the cosmos were connected. The techniques of astrology were very much aimed at determining the human's context within society and the world, and their good or bad fortune therein.

Looking back at how the worldview of the Western world evolved through the centuries, I think that the increasing movement away from the gods and a mythic sense of universe, and towards a more abstract emphasis on Reason as a way of apprehending divine order, carried the earliest roots of what became a complete split within the human psyche in later history.

Astrology flowered at a time when the world of Math and Reason, and the world of Myth and of the Gods, were still alive and integrated.

The context of modern astrology

Much of modern astrology is placed within a context borrowed from Eastern Philosophy. This goes back to Alan Leo, who did much to shape early 20th century astrology as emphasizing character analysis. Leo was a Theosophist, and much of his metaphysic goes back to Blavatsky's version of Hindu cosmology.

More recently you have astrologers like Jeff Green of Evolutionary Astrology looking to Indian teachers like Paramahansa Yogananda for their spiritual context.

Traditional astrology is part of a movement to recover the Western philosophical and spiritual roots of the astrology that developed in the West. Along with a recovery of traditional techniques, there is a renewed interest in recovering the Greek and Roman philosophical roots that underlay the system.

So, among other differences, much of 20th century astrology looks to the East for its spiritual roots. Practitioners of traditional Western astrology are more likely to look back to the Greek and Roman philosophical tradition for its context and roots.

Chapter Four:
The Worldview of Traditional Astrology

In this chapter I would like to give you a feel for the worldview of traditional astrology. This is to give you a sense for how traditional astrologers viewed the planets, and how they act within our world.

Consider approaching this section as a thought experiment. Our modern worldview is very different from what I describe here, so taking a few moments to enter into this older world in your imagination will help you understand the world that gave rise to astrology.

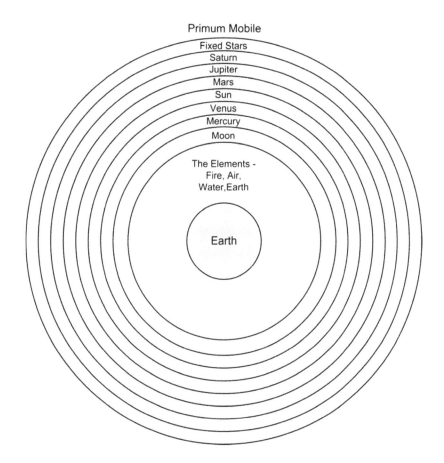

Figure 1: The Traditional Model of the World

The worldview of traditional astrology is geocentric. The earth is at the center of the universe, and around it there is a big bowl, a vast closed dome, cavern or sphere, called the firmament in the opening chapter of Genesis in the Bible.

The outermost ring of this cavern is the Prime Mover, or Primum Mobile, source of all, eternal, and the realm of the highest deity. Just within that is a sphere of the fixed stars. They were called fixed because it was thought that they never changed their position in the dome relative to each other. Hence they were fixed in position like lights attached to the dome.

Within the sphere of the fixed stars, there were spots in the sky that changed their position over time. These are the planets, from the Greek phrase *aster planetes*, meaning wandering star. Each of the seven classical planets, including the two Lights, the Sun and moon, has their own sphere or orbit around the earth. The planets are like lesser gods or mediator beings that transmit the will of deity from the primum mobile down into our sphere of the earth. Each planet has its own domain of responsibility and its own way of acting. Each of the planets inhabits its own ring or heaven counting outward from the earth, with Saturn being the seventh heaven, the outermost before the realm of the fixed stars.

In the realm of the stars and planets all is eternal. The movement is orderly, regular, and predictable.

The planet closest to the earth is our Moon. Within the moon's orbit, is the sublunary sphere, the realm of change, of birth, growth, decay and death. This is the realm of the four ancient elements, fire, air, water and earth. The elements are in four rings inside the Moon's orbit, with fire outermost, then air, then water, and earth, the densest of the elements, at the center. It is the interaction and transformation of the elements that causes change on earth. The planets act on and affect the realm of the elements, and each planet has its own elemental affinity.

As the cavernous bowl of the fixed stars rotates around the earth, the moving planets have their own course around the earth, a daily movement, and a change in position relative to the fixed stars through time. The band in which the planets move is called the Ecliptic, and it is that band that is divided up into 12 equal sized sections that we refer to as the signs of the Zodiac.

At the time of a person's birth, their natal chart is defined by whatever part of the bowl of the Zodiac was coming up over the horizon right at birth. The word Horoscope is from the Greek *horoscopos* or hour marker, and it originally referred to just the rising point in the Zodiac that we now refer to as the Ascendant.

The highest point in the sky that the Sun reaches in the day marks the location of the Midheaven. In the natal chart, that particular configuration of the Zodiac with a specific degree at the Ascendant and another at the Midheaven, is divided up into 12 sections that are what we refer to as the Houses of the chart. The Zodiac and the signs are universal. The ascendant, midheaven and houses are personal, and refer to the special configuration of the Zodiac and planets at the time and place of the native's birth. That snapshot of the dome of the heavens, with the fixed stars and the movable planets, is a picture of the native's personal place within the order of the cosmos.

Because the realm of the planets and fixed stars is eternal, there are orderly and predicable rules for their movement around the earth. It is an intricate geometric system describing the positions of the planets and stars, their relations to each other, and how those positions and relations signified certain kinds of happenings here on earth.

It is that correlation between the position and movement of the planets and stars, and circumstances on earth that is traditional astrology.

This is a closed, geometrically orderly universe, where everything including us has its place, and the planets mediate the will of the highest eternal heaven down to earth. The whole concept of not belonging is unthinkable; the question is not, "Do I have a place?", but rather, "Where is my ordained place?". A person did not attempt to bend the world to do their will. Instead, they worked to discover and to fill their place within the order. Even a conqueror like Alexander the Great had been favored by the Gods to accomplish what he did - the Gods smiled upon them.

Sometimes they frowned. Not fun, but part of the order of the universe.

Astrology in the Modern World

We no longer live in a fixed universe, where the earth is at the unmoving center and all of creation revolves around humanity's special place at the center of creation.

More importantly, we have lost the sense of connection between the outer order of the material universe, and the inner universe of meaning and values. We are isolated and meaningless specks, living on a tiny planet moving swiftly around the Sun that is itself moving within the larger solar system.

The sense of the overall coherency of creation has been lost.

We still do inhabit an ordered worldview. The movements of the planets and stars from our perspective here on earth is completely ordered and predictable, so much so that we can have ephemerides for thousands of years that are accurate to within a few minutes for the planet's position.

But, we have lost any sense of connection between that external order, and the internal order and meaning of our lives.

Practicing astrology helps to recover that sense of order, the correspondence between outer events and inner significance.

The earth is not the fixed center of the universe. But, neither is any other point. All are in motion. No one point is the single fixed measuring point.

We as humans live here on earth. We are looking out at the planets and stars from our particular point of view, and that is what is measured in geocentric astrology. Astrology interprets the meaning of the universe from our particular position, from our point of view.

Traditional astrology can help us recover a sense of the planets as active agents, Gods if you will, having rulership or responsibility over different aspects of existence within an overall ordered whole that includes the outer world of events, and our inner world of meaning. I think this helps keep us from viewing the planets too glibly or abstractly, or taking a shallow or reductionist view of how they act.

I like to use the term Gods to apply to the planets to remind myself I am dealing with what seem to be living, conscious and autonomous entities that I need to interact with and comes to terms with. In this context I deliberately capitalize the word Gods to indicate the same level of reverence that is accorded the singular noun, God. I think a certain amount of holy awe is appropriate when dealing with astrology in general and the planets in particular. I find that perspective to be both realistic and practical.

Thinking of the planets as living Gods within a larger order can be a useful metaphor for recovering a sense of overall order and meaning within ourselves and within the larger cosmos.

There is something very powerful about really confronting the Gods of the planets, seeing them at work in your own life, and getting a sense of them as larger living powers in your life.

Astrology is distinctly sacred, and gives a glimpse into a larger order, a sense of our being part of a world in which we are operating with, and being operated on by, distinctly larger numinous forces that I have been calling the Gods of the planets. I'm laying out this sense of the traditional astrology world order to give a feel for this larger cosmic order that we are all part of, to give a sense of the planet's aliveness.

I also want to give a sense that the planets are very much alive and seem to wish to communicate with us. I get the distinct sense that the chart has a message that it is trying to get across to me, or using me as astrologer to get a necessary message across to a client. Having a reverent attitude towards the planets as intelligences that wish to communicate with us and act on and within our world seems to enhance the quality of that communication.

There is a predictive aspect to astrology, but there is also an interactive and communicative aspect, in which the process of getting in touch with the planets and their actions in our lives, sets up an interactive communication that helps to shape events. The world does not just act on us; we do not just shape and create our world; there is an interactive, inter-communicating, participatory dance that seems to take place, and our lives are shaped by how we participate in that dance.

The world of all of astrology, both traditional and modern, is larger than we are, and the powers represented by the planets act on us and through us, in all aspects of our existence, internal and external. To paraphrase Martha Lynn-Wescott, the planets will tend to have an effect on every possible level.

When you turn your attention to reading an astrology chart, particularly if you are an astrologer working with a receptive client   take off your shoes and tremble; you are on holy ground, so tread lightly and with care.

Chapter Five:
The Language of Traditional Astrology

Approaching reading the older texts

When you first start to study some of the oldest astrology texts, they come across as quite fatalistic, black and white, good and evil, extreme good fortune and extreme bad fortune.

I think that the older texts, like Dorotheus, Ptolemy and Paul of Alexandria, are best read as suggestive aphorisms or seed-thoughts for a kind of contemplation. The language is image-rich and concrete, much less vague and abstract than much modern astrological writing.

Take a text like Dorotheus and try to read it straight through like modern prose, and it can be either tedious or confusing. Slow down and dwell on the individual groups of thoughts and images, and it is very rich and fruitful.

Read a modern astrology book on a planet and you will get a definition. Read a traditional text and you get a string of anecdotes, things, places, and events. This is like describing a person by bringing up your memories of them, what they did, what they looked like, their quirks, their habits, and so on.

(Quote from Avraham Ivn Ezra, The Book of Reasons, 11th century, p 29-30)

> "Jupiter indicates wisdom and worship of God for he is temperate... His is the liver, because it is the source of blood, which is warm and moist... He signifies the king's counselor for he is loyal, and when with Mars, he indicates a wealthy person for he signifies money, and Mars signifies tax collector. When with Venus he is the songs. When Mercury transfers his influence to him, he indicates knowledge of the law and serving justice, or when with the Sun, for the Sun is the sovereign of the planets."

(Quote from Dorotheus (very influential early Greek astrologer) on conjunctions with Saturn p 221)

> "If Saturn is with Jupiter, he will abound in landed estates and will be the steward for kings and nobles, entrusted with properties other than his own, and he will be noble if Mars does not aspect it. If Saturn is with Mars, it indicates good in his character, but there will be no good in regard to his property, and reason will keep him waiting, and he will marry, and his body will be weakened, and his bile and black bile will be aroused against him, and his father will die before his mother...if Jupiter aspects, it will make easy and dissipate this misery and he will bear it."

In order to understand the language, you unpack the images and attempt to think through *why* that particular event is associated with that planet in that condition or that house. The symbols of astrology - planets, signs, houses, aspects, dignities and so on - take on a concrete richness that escapes the attempt to classify them.

The planets are not convenient signs for abstract keywords. They are multifaceted, living symbols, living beings - in older language, gods - and they are richer in meaning than anything we can put into language. The images of concrete events bring the symbols more alive.

To give you an example of how older language differs from our abstract modern norm, consider this modern bible translation of Luke 1:51 from Mary's Magnificat :

> He has scattered the proud in their conceit.

Now, here is the same verse from the King James Version of 1611 -

> He hath scattered the proud in the imagination of their hearts.
> *(Note - scattered has 3 syllables, and is pronounced something like, sca-te-red - it rolls off the tongue.)*

They both convey about the same meaning, but the modern version is thinner and more vaguely abstract, and the second older version is richer, more concrete.

In order to study older traditional astrology texts, you will need to come to terms with that older, richer language.

It is worth noting that the descriptions of the planets in older text are often in extremes, either in very good condition or very bad. The effect of planets, most of the time, is somewhere in-between extremes. The extreme examples are very rarely predictive as is, but they do give a very vivid picture of the meaning and working of the planet.

Section Two: Building Blocks

Chapter Six:
The Building Blocks - Introduction

Before we can examine the Planets, Signs and Houses, there are some root concepts of the traditional astrology worldview that we need to look at. I call them the Building Blocks.

First, we need to get very clear that the Hellenistic concept of how the world was created is almost exactly the opposite of ours. In the modern scientific worldview the universe is built up from matter, which forms patterns that become more complex. To a scientist, the physical brain is what gives rise to our consciousness, so the mind is rooted in matter.

To the ancient Greeks, the Mind came first, and the Body second. The universe for them is created from living Ideas. These ideas then take on matter and form and become manifest - the Word becomes flesh and dwells among us. They started with simpler or more fundamental ideas, and viewed more complex ideas and beings as being built up from those simple core qualities. The simpler an Idea was, the closer it was to the heart of the Divine Pattern.

To the Greeks, learning and contemplating these building block concepts was like having a peek into God's workshop, in which we get a glimpse behind the curtain and watch the Universe being created.

To a Pythagorean mystic, contemplating the number 3 would call forth the same sort of reverence and awe that a Catholic would feel before an image of the Blessed Virgin. (I would imagine that many modern scientists feel the same about their mathematical formulas.)

The patterns of numbers, of geometry, of the elements and so on, are both organizing concepts, and they are also living patterned forces that bring those concepts into manifestation. We are learning what they considered to be a pre-existing and living Sacred Science that was a gift to humanity.

Please remove your shoes and take a minute to compose your mind; we are about to take our first steps into the Sacred Temple.

Chapter Seven:
Astrology and Sacred Geometry

Astrology as we know it is part of a grand synthesis of elements from Babylonian and Egyptian culture, fused together into a new whole during the peak of Hellenistic culture.

A crucial part of that synthesis is the geometry. This is the period of the Pythagorean schools, which had a strong element of number and geometry symbolism in their approach to the sacred.

The discovery of the elegant symmetry and organization of geometry and mathematics was considered a window into the sacred order of the Universe, and was given the sort of reverence and awe that we associate with religion.

So, part of the sacred discipline of astrology is a geometric order that ties the system together, and that has meaning in itself.

In our modern astrology we tend to think of the meaning largely in mythological terms, and the mathematical calculations and geometric structure are viewed as something you need to do to get at the mythology. In truth, the Math and the Meaning are completely intertwined. The better you understand the math and geometry, the more the entire system takes on added meaning.

Number and Geometry were considered especially sacred because they are so fundamental, such very pure and basic qualities. They are primitive in the sense of being very basic, foundational, and primitive as in prime, near the first, the source or the core.

I want to present two related diagrams here to give a window into that sacred order. There is a sense in which these diagrams provide a kind of framework for the entire system that we will be examining. I am presenting it at this early point in the book to give the rest of the concepts a geometric shape or container, a visual image you can use to help organize the system of traditional astrology in your mind.

As we go over the geometry, consider viewing these diagrams as sacred mandalas and as a focus for meditation.

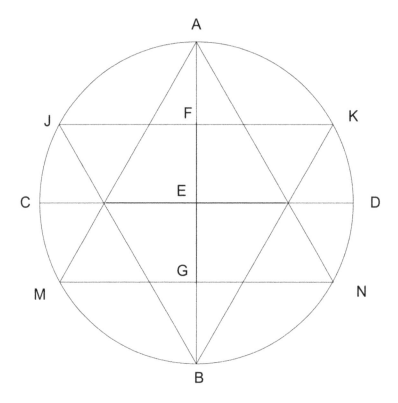

Figure 2: The Geometry of the Aspects

This diagram gives an idea of the geometry that is behind dividing the Zodiac into twelve parts, and how the aspects are defined.

 In order to create this diagram, you first start with a circle, and divide it in 4 with a cross (lines AB and CD).

Next, take the vertical arm of the cross, which is a diameter of the circle, and divide each vertical arm in half a second time (at points F and G), so the vertical line is now divided into four equal segments.

Finally, use the two division points to draw a pair of horizontal lines. Each one of these new horizontal lines will be one of 3 sides of an equilateral triangle pointing up (AMN) or down (BJK).

Just contemplate that for a moment - taking the diameter of a circle and dividing it in 4 equal parts defines the sides of 2 equilateral triangles touching the circle's circumference that converge on the 2 ends of the defining diameter. ***The number 4 gives us 2, 3-sided figures.*** For people who viewed numbers as living, numinous entities, this intertwining of the numbers 2, 3 and 4 would have been viewed as a revelation of order in the Mind of God. The elegance is breathtaking, and this diagram can be a fruitful subject for meditation.

The points where the cross and those 2 triangles touch the circle define the Ptolemaic aspects - 60 degrees (angle AK), a sextile, and 120 degrees (angle AN), a trine, for the triangles, 90 degrees (angle AD), a square, and 180 degrees (angle AB), an opposition, for the crosses. The missing 30 degree increments, 30 and 150, (which modern astrologers call semisextile and inconjunct), are the angles that are considered to be averse or not aspecting each other, and hence are not considered aspects in the traditional sense. *(This will be discussed further in the chapter on aspects.)*

The points of the triangles, related to the number 3, define the benefic, smooth or positive aspects. The points of the cross, related to the number 4, define the malefic, stressful or negative aspects.

Add the 2 sideways equilateral triangles and you get the 30 degree divisions of the 12 houses or 12 signs of the Zodiac.

Note: *The modern aspect system is based on an entirely different geometric model that goes back to Kepler. This does not mean that modern aspect theory does not work; just that it is based on an entirely different geometric model than traditional astrology. I personally use both traditional and modern aspects, but I give them somewhat different meanings.*

The Stakes

This is a major interpretive structure that you will see referred to repeatedly in traditional texts. It is an expression of the number 4, and is related to that basic cross in the circle on which everything else is built. Four is the number of form, manifestation, matter, also tension, instability and stress.

The stakes are the 90 degree angles, the cross, formed by a sign, and by the signs opposite it and at right angles to it. When interpreting the meaning of a planet or house, you first look at what other planets are in the stakes relative to that planet. You will see, when we discuss the major aspects, that any planet in the stakes to another planet is in either whole sign square or opposition, both of which are powerful and significant.

So, the structure of the stakes, that cross shape, defines the area of greatest activity affecting a point.

In the Zodiac, it is defined by opposite signs by degrees of longitude on ecliptic.

In an individual native's horoscope, the axes of the Ascendant /Descendant line, and the Midheaven /Immum Coeli line, define the stakes of the chart, and they are the points of the greatest power and activity of planets in the chart.

Chapter Eight:
The Thema Mundi

That basic structure based on the numbers 3, 4, and 6, gives us the 12 section division we associate with the Zodiac. This next diagram takes that geometry and combines it with the symbolism of the planets and stars. It is called the Thema Mundi, and in some ways this diagram is a synthesis of the entire system. It is a very fruitful source for ongoing contemplation and will yield increasing richness of meaning over time.

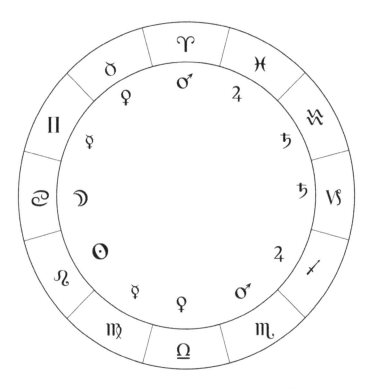

Figure 3: Thema Mundi with Rulerships

The Thema Mundi is a kind of mandala, a foundation pattern or teaching device, and is also fruitful focus for contemplation or meditation.

It is described as being a chart of the mythical beginning of the world. This was probably not taken to be literally true. Most likely it was created as a teaching tool from the beginning.

Note that the Thema puts the sign Cancer on the Ascendant as the first house. The start of the sign Cancer is the Summer Solstice, the hottest time of the year, the time of the triumph of the lights. The 2 lights, the Sun and Moon, are the rulers of the first two signs from the Ascendant, Cancer and Leo. Around them on either side are the other planets taking pairs of signs in the order of their distance from the Sun.

You have Sun and Moon, then on either side of them are Mercury, then Venus, then Mars, Jupiter, and finally Saturn. The symmetry shows the sign rulership of all of the planets. Sun and Moon each rule one sign, all the other planets rule two each.

So you have a symmetry of planets around the Moon and the Sun, the 2 lights.

The lights rule the first two summer signs, Cancer and Leo, the time of the greatest light.

Saturn, lord of darkness, is opposite the 2 lights. While the Lights take the two summer months, Saturn takes the months of greatest cold and darkness, ruling the winter signs Capricorn and Aquarius.

Thema Mundi and the Aspects

Along with showing sign rulerships, the Thema Mundi also shows the nature of the different aspects, by the position of the planets relative to the two Lights.

Please see the diagram on the following page, which shows how the meanings of the aspects are derived from the positions of the planets in the order of the Thema Mundi.

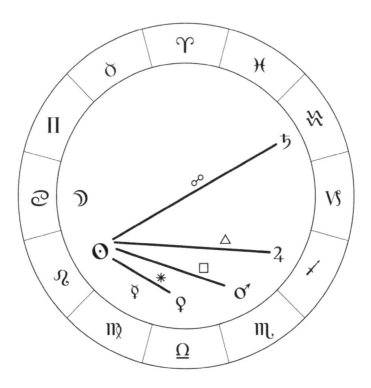

Figure 4: Thema Mundi with Aspects

Venus in Libra is Sextile the Sun in Leo, so the sextile is of the nature of Venus.

Mars in Scorpio is square to the Sun in Leo, so the square is of the nature of Mars.

Jupiter is in Sagittarius which trines the Sun in Leo, so the trine is of the nature of Jupiter .

And finally, Saturn in Aquarius is opposite the Sun in Leo, so the opposition is of the nature of Saturn.

Chapter Nine:
Organizing Concepts

With the geometry and the Thema Mundi we have a sense of order, but it is static, unmoving. To understand the Universe we need to set order into motion, and have concepts that help us to understand that moving order. We have considered Space, and now we need to introduce Time.

There are two main organizing concepts that work together in traditional astrology. I want to look at them together to provide a conceptual framework for understanding this system.

First, we have repeating cycles, birth, growth, flourishing, decline, decay, and death.

Astrology is cyclical. I need to emphasize this, since our modern worldview is not. Our modern worldview is based on a profoundly religious belief in progress which goes in a straight line. This is such an all-pervasive belief in western culture that even many modern astrologers have an unspoken assumption that the progress of a chart in time is related to an ongoing, ever increasing progress of evolution of the individual. We breathe belief in progress the way we invisibly breathe air.

And second, we have complementary and alternating pairs of opposites.

Astrology works with a core set of alternating pairs of opposites - day and night, masculine and feminine, cold and hot, dry and wet, and so on. We will examine some of those when we explore the symbolism of the number two.

Opposites and Cycles work together

The pairs of opposites alternate in cycles - day is followed by night. Growth is followed by decline. Youth is followed by age. Birth is followed by death.

In astrology we have day and night, summer and winter. Days get longer, days get shorter. Plants sprout, bloom, grow and die, just as the Moon is reborn each month, grows to full, then declines and dies again.

In our modern linear worldview we tend to not understand the cyclical nature of much of our world.

We accept growth, but not decline. Witness the desperate efforts to keep the economy in a perpetual state of growth. It is just assumed or believed that the economy should always naturally be expanding and growing, and any interruption of that growth is viewed as a temporary aberration or setback.

In the natural world, with any kind of living being or ecosystem, perpetual growth is both monstrous and impossible.

We accept youth, but not aging, so we encourage the natural process of growth and do all we can to fight or deny the equally natural process of aging. We accept life, but not death, so birth is welcomed and celebrated, while death is denied, fought and hidden.

In astrology the movement is circular, cyclical, and not linear. There is no straight line growth. There is birth, but there is death. There is youth, there is age.

These cycles of life are mirrored in the cycles of the planets. For instance, just as there is birth, growth, decline and death, we have the phases of the Moon, from the birth at new and growth to full, through the decline of the waning Moon and the death/rebirth at the new Moon. Other planets have similar cycles.

There are planets that build up, and we call them benefic. There are planets that obstruct and break down, and we call them malefic. Each is a necessary part of a full cycle.

It is important to reflect that, when you view a chart, you are not looking at *only* possibilities for growth. You are also looking at possibilities for decline. Possibilities for success, and possibilities for failure. Possibilities for good and bad fortune.

Note that even those humanistic astrologers, working in the stream of practice that goes back to Dane Rudhyar, tend to talk about their cycles in the context of an ongoing process of evolution which is ever-ascending. You don't have growth and decline, you have growth that leads to... further growth ad infinitum. For me that is not what is truly meant by the term cyclical. A spiral is straight line evolution in disguise.

It is true that no two cycles are quite identical, and that the events of one cycle do influence the events of the following cycle. It is also true that we, as human beings, can have a process of learning that goes on through the cycles. However, even that process of learning is part of a larger process of mental growth and decline. It is conceivable that this decline is part of a seed that becomes a new life or growth after what we think of as death, but that does not mean that we can skip over the human physical reality of growth, decline and death.

If there is a single perspective that defines traditional astrology as distinct from much modern astrology, it is this acceptance of the full, balanced cycle of growth and decline, life and death, benefic and malefic, with all conditions and stages in between.

Chapter Ten:
Number Symbolism

Astrology and Number Symbolism

We have established the fact that traditional astrology is built on a structured world of geometry and number.

In this worldview, numbers are not just a way to measure, calculate or count. Numbers have meaning and quality, and each number is unique. Also, the numbers are alive, numinous, living entities from within the Mind of God.

The number 2 is much more than 1+1, or one less than 3. It is a living being in its own right, having its own personality, its own qualities, its own characteristic meaning and flavor.

Since numbers are such simple, primitive ideas, their being and meaning pervade and determine the elaborate astrological structures we build upon them. The system of astrology in its entirety can get quite complicated, but getting the sense of the meaning of just a few core numbers helps to simplify understanding the entire system.

So, before we look at anything else, we need to take a moment to meet the numbers.

The Key numbers are 2, 3, and 4. All others build from them.

The Number 2

The number two is the number of division, of duality, of separation. There can be no manifestation without separation. Undifferentiated Unity is unthinkable because there is no difference within it to conceive.

Two connotes awareness of the Other. There can be no awareness, no consciousness as we normally use the term, without an other to be aware of.

The other can be a partnership, but it can also be an opponent.

It is very important to realize that this does not mean just that "I see myself reflected in the other". This means, "I see an other who is not me." It may indeed be true that I see aspects of myself reflected in others, but this cannot happen unless there actually are others for me to interact with.

The number two also connotes balancing pairs. And, when set in motion, two connotes a cycle where opposites alternate. They can be complementary, or contrasting, or opposed.

Two is also the tension or stress of opposites.

Two can also be contrasting or balancing qualities.

We will see the number two come into play in the various pairs of opposites - day and night, benefic and malefic, masculine and feminine, active and passive, and so on.

The Number 3

The number 3 is used in astrology in a couple of different ways, one of them static, and one of them dynamic.

The number three as a static structure, a triangle, is two opposites balanced and joined by a third point in the center that combines and harmonizes them.

Within diversity, it gives a Unity of opposites joined. The geometric structure of 3 is a triangle, which is a stable structure. The number 3 connotes stability, smoothness, ease.

In the process of manifestation, 3 is Idea is contrasted with 4 as Matter.

But, 3 comes after 1 and 2 - after separation - so it implies unity after division.

In a static sense, we see the number three in the aspect called the Trine, which is considered the smoothest, most stable and most favorable of the aspects.

Looking at the number 3 as parts of a process, we get three stages initiation and first growth, followed by a sustained and mature period, and finally a final period of decay, wavering, change, and instability which is both an ending, and a transition to the start of a new cycle of growth, maturity, decline and transition.

The number three in astrology is reflected in two important three part cycles - the modes of cardinal, fixed and mutable for the Signs, and angular, succedent and cadent for the houses.

Notice that the main cyclic divisions of 3 - the modes and angularity - imply a movement in time, a repeating cycle of change. Since 3 is a number associated with stability, in a dynamic sense we can view that stability in predictable cycles of change.

The Number 4

The number 4, which is 2 times 2, is a number of manifestation, matter and instability. I want to emphasize that - the number of matter is unstable and tense!

Rectangles and squares are inherently unstable, and that is why 4 is matter - not because of stability, what we might call solidity, but because it is unstable.

To see the difference in stability between the numbers 3 and 4, consider building a triangle out of soda straws held together by twine or thread through them. The triangle is stable; it keeps its shape. By contrast, if you build a 4 sided figure with 4 straws and twine, it will not keep its shape; it flops all over the place.

Ideas are stable, matter is unstable.

With the number 4 we have stress, stability, tension, movement.

The symbolism of the number 4 is found in the 4 elements, and the related 4 seasons of the year, and 4 types of temperament. There are also 4 quadrants in house division, and the 4 signs in opposition or square to each other, forming a cross, are referred to as the Stakes. The aspects related to the number 4 are stressful and unstable.

Now that we have met the numbers, we are ready to consider the world that is built up with them. We need to give the numbers flesh and form; we need to start by clothing them in the four elements.

Chapter Eleven:
The Four elements

Introduction

The elements are built up out of the numbers 2 and 4. Two is that first act of division into complementary pairs of opposites, and connotes relationship, opposition, balance, and also change by alternation.

The number 4, the number of physical matter, gives us a physical structure, but one that is unstable, tense, constantly changing and shifting.

When we talk about the world of the elements, we are in that realm called sublunary, within the orbit of the moon. Outside of the ring of the moon all is ordered and stable; within that order all is shifting instability and change. It is the mutable world of earth that we call home.

The four elements in astrology are made up of the 4 qualities, in two pairs - hot and cold, and moist and dry. We will first examine the qualities, then combine them to look at the elements.

Hot and cold are considered to be active qualities, moist and dry are considered passive.

Table 1: Hot and Cold - Table of Qualities

Hot	Cold
moves up	moves down
expands	contracts
active	passive
moves forward	retreats
speeds up	slows down
advances	withdraws
adventurous, optimistic	cautious, pessimistic
diurnal	nocturnal

Hot and cold are the two opposite kinds of motions, like the rhythm of breathing out and breathing in. Hot is a motion that moves up, forward and outward, and cold retreats, pulls in, and retracts. It's like the difference between summer and winter - our bodies open and expand into the heat, and withdraw and contract to protect from the chill.

Table 2: Moist and Dry - Table of Qualities

Moist	Dry
connects	separates
flexible	rigid
softens	hardens
receptive	unreceptive
blurs distinctions	accentuates distinctions

Moist and dry are a different kind of pair. They are related to the movement of coming together and of separating. We talk of bare bones or dry facts when we want to look at things distinctly, to separate them. Adding moistness connects, but it also blurs. When things dry up they are lifeless; we need to add moisture to reconnect and form new life or sustain existing life.

Now take those two pairs, combine them in the 4 possible ways, and you get the 4 elements.

Table 3: Elements by Quality

	Dry	Moist
Hot	fire	air
Cold	earth	water

Given those basic qualities, we will now examine the four elements in turn.

Fire - *hot and dry* - active, optimistic, moving, and ascending. A good element to get things done, or at least get things started. At the same time, the dry aspect of fire can make it rigid, not always flexible, drawing boundaries, making distinctions. Fire is considered diurnal.

Fire is active, but it needs but it needs air, and it needs earth, the most passive of elements, to feed on. Fire signs can provide energy, but they can also feed on, and burn up, the people around them.

Fire is light, so it is related to vision, seeing.

Fire is active but not reflective, not self-aware. Also, fire moves quickly.

Water - *cold and moist* - passive, receptive, cautious and descending. Water flows in all directions and takes the shape of whatever container it is in. It is a good element to slow down, pause, meditate, draw inward, and connect things, smooth off hard corners. Planets in water are more sensitive, emotional, introspective, receptive, and internal. Water is considered nocturnal. Also, water is reflective.

Water flows downward as opposed to fire flowing upward. So, fire tends to be more optimistic, water tends to be more pessimistic or cautious.

Air - *hot and moist* - combines some of the activity of fire with the connectivity of water. Air also 'flows' but outward rather than downward, and tends to escape out of containers. Air connects by moving sideways, blowing where it will. Air is associated with intellect, communication, exchange of ideas. Air, being warm and active, is considered diurnal. Air is a social and mental element.

Earth - *cold and dry* - rigid, stable, passive, unyielding, but also supportive. Provides the shape, the container - without earth the other elements would have no way to keep a shape. When completely dry, earth is hard. It takes water to soften and loosen the earth, make it pliable. Too much water and earth loses its dry quality, and its shape, altogether, and can be washed away. Earth is associated with material reality, practicality. Earth can also be sensual, in touch with the body. Earth also slows down any planets in it. Earth, being passive, is considered nocturnal.

These 4 qualities are looked at as pairs of opposites.
- Fire boils water, water extinguishes fire.
- Earth contains or blocks air, air flows around or disperses earth.

The elements are not stable and static conditions. They are continually mixing, blending, changing. The four seasons are an image of the four elements set into cyclic motion, transforming one into the other. They seasons take the elements and combine them with the process of time.

The Elements and the Seasons

The 4 seasons

The two warm seasons are diurnal - day is longer than night. The two cold seasons are nocturnal - night is longer than day.

Each of the seasons in turn has one quality that is dominant, and another that is increasing in strength, that then leads into the next season. In each of the seasons in order a single quality shifts.

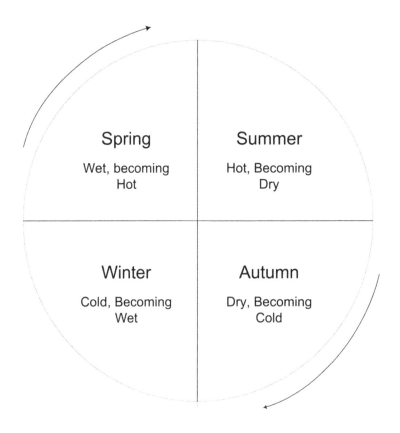

Figure 5: The Cycle of the Seasons

Spring, which is air, is hot and moist. Hot is increasing during the spring, which tends to dry things out.

Summer is quite hot and dry, but the dryness leads to cooling off in autumn.

Autumn is cold and dry, but as things get colder they get wetter.

Winter is cold and wet, and the wetness leads to heat increasing in the spring, and so on.

The four elements move through the seasons in an ongoing, repeating cycle, where each transforms into the next by its imbalance. This is very similar to the Chinese Tai Chi symbol, where yin and yang alternate by transforming into each other.

The Elements and the Planets

The basic definitions of the planets are *partly* derived from their elemental structure. The elemental makeup of a planet helps to explain how it functions. The planet is not reducible just to its elemental quality, but that quality is an important part of the planet's identity. It says a lot about how that planet functions in the realm of the elements, what its affinities are.

There are some disagreements and inconsistencies in the attributions of the elements to the planets. The ones that I am using here go back to Ptolemy.

While we will examine the planets in more detail a little later, I want to briefly go over them here and examine them just in terms of the 4 qualities, hot, cold, moist, and dry.

Table 4: Planets by Element

Planet	Elemental Makeup
Sun	moderately hot and dry
Moon	very cold and moist
Mercury	varies by position
Venus	moderately cool and moist
Mars	very hot and dry
Jupiter	moderately warm and moist
Saturn	very cold and dry

The Sun is moderately hot and dry - it is life-giving, but can be harmful. When a planet gets too close to the Sun it is considered to be Combust or burnt up by the Sun, which is one of the most debilitating conditions a planet can be in.

The Moon is cold and moist, passive, receptive. It is considered to be the wettest planet.

Jupiter and Venus are both moderate, and both moist. Jupiter is moist and moderately hot, Venus is moist and usually described as cold, or rather, cool. Jupiter is moist in an expansive, outgoing way. Venus is moist in a cool, receptive way.

Some traditional sources show Jupiter as cool and moist, and Venus as warm and moist. Both are considered as moderate either way. I think it makes more sense to make Jupiter warm since it goes with the expansiveness, and Venus cool since it goes with a more passive receptiveness. Also, Jupiter is a warm day planet, and Venus is a cool night planet.

Mars and Saturn are both extremes - Mars is extreme hot and dry, Saturn is extreme cold and dry. Both are threatening because of their very imbalance and extremeness.

Mercury, again, is considered to be ambivalent. It is sometimes described as natively cool and dry. Some say it changes depending on whether it rises before or after the Sun.

Also - important - it is very common to say that Mercury takes on the characteristics of the planet(s) it most closely aspects - notice, not the sign it is in, but the planets it aspects, which is an example in traditional astrology of planets being more important than signs. Realistically, in my experience, the meaning of Mercury needs to take both sign and aspected planets into account.

The Elements and the Zodiac

The 12 signs are divided up into four groups, with three signs being given to each of the four elements. This is where we are mapping the realm of the elements onto the geometry of the circle divided into 12 by triangle and cross.

Table 5: Zodiac Signs by Element

fire	Aries, Leo, Sagittarius
water	Cancer, Scorpio, Pisces
air	Libra, Aquarius, Gemini
earth	Capricorn, Taurus, Virgo

We will examine the signs of the Zodiac in detail in a later section.

Chapter Twelve:
Benefic and Malefic

So far we have seen that much of astrology is built up from from simple pairs of complementary and alternating opposites.

There is another primary pair of opposites, very important in chart evaluation, and that is benefic and malefic. Benefic means beneficial, malefic means harmful. This has nothing to do with good or evil, or even whether things eventually 'work out for the best'.

Benefic is related to building up, malefic is related to building down. They are complementary and necessary parts of a whole cycle.

There are two benefic planets, Jupiter and Venus. The two malefic planets are Saturn and Mars.

We usually experience the benefic planets as pleasant, comfortable, growing, and life-enhancing. We experience the malefic planets as extreme, unpleasant, challenging, dangerous, and threatening.

As we will see later, a lot depends on the dignity or condition of the specific planet. Saturn in good shape can have a benefic effect, and Jupiter in bad shape can have a malefic effect.

Jupiter, the greater benefic, and Venus, the lesser benefic, are both moderate in their elemental makeup. Their effect tends to be to build up, expand, combine, relate, interconnect, and grow. We usually experience their effect as pleasant, enjoyable - as good in the usual sense of the term.

Saturn, the greater malefic, and Mars, the lesser malefic, are both extreme in their elemental makeup - Saturn is extreme cold and dry, Mars is extreme hot and dry.

Notice that both of the benefics are moist, and both of the malefics are dry. Moist connects and harmonizes, dry separates and distinguishes.

The effect of the malefics, Mars and Saturn, tends to be to disrupt, block, separate, contract or cut, decay, fall apart, die. We usually experience their effect as unpleasant - bad in the ordinary sense of the term. All kinds of no fun.

I'm writing this paragraph in Minnesota in January during a cold winter, and the air temperature outside is twenty degrees Fahrenheit below zero with a stiff wind. That is cold and dry Saturn to an extreme. To call the weather evil would be silly, but it sure isn't any fun. In late July I can look forward to high temperatures around a hundred degrees with high humidity. That is the Sun being extremely hot to the point of being malefic. Again, not evil, but no fun. That is malefic.

This does NOT mean that life would be better if the two malefics weren't around. Jupiter without Saturn would mean unbounded growth. We need growth and expansion, but we also need the balance of decay, contraction, limitation. We need birth, but we also need that to be balanced by death.

The fine traditional astrologer Robert Zoller makes the important point that we as astrologers need the categories of benefic and malefic while evaluating a chart, but that does not mean that these terms or their meanings are for the client to hear. I think you can make a case for presenting negative conditions to a client in a way they would find helpful, but that is a completely separate issue from how we evaluate the chart.

Positive/Negative evaluation

Tied in with the paired concepts of benefic and malefic, it is common for traditional astrology to approach evaluating a chart with lists of conditions that were considered positive or benefic, and a matching list of conditions considered negative or malefic. (**Note**: *We will examine such a list in a later chapter.*) Evaluating a chart meant going through those conditions to see how a planet or point balanced out. If all the conditions were negative a planet's action would be considered extremely malefic, and the opposite if all the conditions were positive. Usually the actual condition was somewhere in the middle, so a weighing and balancing process is part of the final judgment.

Balance and Imbalance

In traditional astrology, benefic conditions are balanced, moderate, while malefic conditions are extreme, out of balance. There was no sense of an extreme polarity of good and evil, but rather the sense that the best conditions were somewhere in a middle position of balance between two opposed extremes.

I want to really emphasize this concept of balance being positive and imbalance being negative, since it is very different from our modern concept of extremes of positive and negative. Let's consider a couple of examples to flesh this out.

In our modern way of thinking, if having $1000 is good, then having $10000 is better, $100,000 way better, and so on. In that model there is no such thing as being rich enough; richer is always better. (Almost everyone in our culture would think, "Well, of course!", and that without a second thought.)

Building a car to be able to drive 50 miles an hour is good, 60 even better, 70 better yet, and so on - the faster the car, the better the car.

Thinking in terms of one-way extremes like this leads to unbalanced thinking, in which other consequences of moving further towards an extreme are usually not considered.

Our culture has lost the sense of balance or a mean as being good, and extremes as being bad. The word **mediocrity** used to have a very positive sense, and meant that perfect place of balance and moderation between extremes. Now we think of mediocrity as lukewarm, inferior, and as a good being something extreme. We've lost our sense of natural balance, and I think that our getting an appreciation for the traditional astrology sense of benefic and malefic can help us get that back.

Chapter Thirteen:
Sect

Much of what we have already explored in astrology is related to the number two, the very basic division into pairs of opposites.

Sect is an expression of one of the most basic divisions in our human experience, the dividing of time into day and night, light and darkness. Things of the day are called diurnal, things of the night are called nocturnal.

Think of them as two opposing teams, or opposing parties in a bipartisan government. In fact, before our age of ubiquitous outer lighting, think about how utterly different the worlds of day and night really are. Think of them like two different realms, with the Sun Lord of the day and the Moon Lady of the night. One is bright, outgoing, visible, and active, the other is dark, inwardly-drawn, invisible, passive, still.

Just as our time is divided into the two realms of day and night, so the planets were divided up into two groups along the same lines.

The day planets are happier and more effective during the day, and the night planets more comfortable at night.

Table 6: Table of Planets by Sect

	Light	Benefic	Malefic
Diurnal	Sun	Jupiter	Saturn
Nocturnal	Moon	Venus	Mars

Mercury can be either, depending on whether it rises before or after Sun. Mercury rising before the Sun, at an earlier Zodiac degree than the Sun, is considered diurnal. Mercury rising after the Sun, at a later Zodiac degree than the Sun, is considered nocturnal.

In a day chart, the day planets will be most comfortable. The night planets are 'out of their element' and not likely to be as balanced or effective. Those conditions are reversed for a night chart.

Notice that the benefic planets are grouped with the sect that harmonizes with their elemental makeup. Jupiter is warm and is grouped with the day, and Venus is cool and is grouped with the night.

By contrast, the two malefic planets are grouped with the sect that contrasts with their elemental makeup, to provide balance. Saturn is cold and dry and is grouped with the day, where its coldness is moderated. Similarly, Mars is hot and dry and is grouped with the night, where the coolness moderates the extreme heat.

When interpreting a chart, other things being equal, you will look for the benefic planet matching the sect of the chart to be the most beneficial, and the malefic planet of the opposite sect to likely be the biggest source of problems.

Whether or not a planet is in sect is a measure of the quality of action of the planet and not of its strength, visibility or ability to act. A planet in sect will be more comfortable, more relaxed, more at home, more balanced, and thus more likely to act in a positive way. By contrast, a planet out of sect is out place, out of its element, unbalanced, tense, edgy, thus more likely to act in a way that causes problems.

Sect measures quality and not power.

Sect was very important, even primary, in Hellenistic astrology, and became less emphasized through the development of astrology. By the time you get to William Lilly and the early Renaissance, sect is of lesser importance; it is no longer a major organizing context. By the twentieth century the concept of sect has pretty much disappeared.

My own experience in reading charts is that sect is indeed important, and colors how effectively a planet acts, but it does not seem to be as primary or important as in the earliest texts. Other factors can weigh heavily to modify that.

As we start to look at other elements of astrology chart symbolism, you will see that they often divide on sect related, diurnal/nocturnal lines.

Other Sect-Related Conditions

There are another two minor sect-related conditions that you will see in some traditional texts.

First, a planet is happiest when it is on the same half of the chart, either upper or lower, as its sect light. The day planets are happiest on the same side of the chart as the Sun, the night planets as the Moon.

Second, the day planets are considered happiest in masculine or diurnal signs, and night planets happiest in feminine or nocturnal signs.

These were minor considerations in Hellenistic astrology, when sect was considered very important, but they took on more importance during the Arabic period.

In this book we will emphasize only the primary consideration of sect, and leave out these minor conditions.

Chapter Fourteen:
Essential Dignities

Introduction

Bring to mind the picture of an ordered cosmos that we've been building here - the carefully structured hierarchical cosmos - each fixed star and wandering planetary star having its own assigned place, in which the 7 planets in their 7 rings or heavens are the mediators of the will of the highest heaven. Think also of the planets each having their assigned houses in the order of the Thema Mundi.

In this model each of the planets is assigned levels of rulership and responsibility of the different sections of the Zodiac through which they travel. Before we can talk about the planets, we need to explore where they fit within the ordered world of number and geometry that we have been exploring.

As the Zodiac is divided into 12 signs by sect, season, element and mode, the planets have their responsibilities and rulerships allotted to different signs, according to the planets' position within the cosmos. Each planet within the living order of the cosmos has a role to play, a duty and responsibility to be carried out. Just as there are multiple levels of order within the cosmos, so the planets have multiple levels of responsibility.

This is the concept of different levels of rulership, what we call the essential dignities of the planets.

Essential dignity does not mean affinity - it means responsibility or ownership.

In a chart, a planet which has rulership over the sign in a given house, is responsible for seeing that the affairs of that house are carried out in the best way possible.

The essential dignity which a planet has determines the general condition or quality of a planet's action.

When a planet is in a sign in which it has essential dignity its actions and affairs will tend to turn out well, in a balanced and controlled way.

Just as there are signs in which planets have dignity and perform well, so there are also signs in which planets do not function well, and these are called debilities.

In an area in which a planet has no dignity or has debility, its actions will turn out poorly, or be imbalanced, or tend to fall apart or otherwise not work out well. Often, the debilitated planet becomes a source of focus or motivation for the native to correct the imbalance, and make it work. For that reason, debilitated planets often are key points to examine.

However, this does not mean that a planet in poor condition in a chart will always be a source of bad fortune. It is common for a debilitated planet in a natal chart to be an area that the native works very hard on, in order to deal with the imbalance or debility. A source of challenge can become a source of strength.

When interpreting a chart, I often find that the planets that are either very dignified or very debilitated are the dominant influences in the overall chart.

Modern astrology has kept two of the dignities, rulership and exaltation, although neither seems to be all that widely used or even taken seriously by some modern astrologers. However, most modern astrologers are aware of the concept of planets ruling some signs, and being exalted in other signs.

Whether they are examined or not, most modern astrology does not emphasize the condition of planets in their interpretation, and that evaluation of condition is the cornerstone of the traditional approach.

As in modern astrology, traditional astrology has two main levels of dignity; rulership, which is also referred to as its domicile or home, and exaltation. They are called the major dignities, and are the most emphasized. In fact, you can do a very good and effective reading using just the two major dignities, and it is worth concentrating on them while you are mastering the system. I will be heavily concentrating on the major dignities in the interpretation example part of this book.

Traditional astrology also has another three levels of minor dignity or rulership, referred to as, triplicity, terms or bounds, and face. After exploring the major dignities, we will look at each of the minor dignities in order.

Different Systems of some of the Dignities

There is broad agreement for the attribution of the major dignities of rulership and exaltation, and for the minor dignity of face. However, for the minor dignities of triplicity and term, there exist multiple versions.

The oldest version of both the triplicities and the terms goes back to Dorotheus of Sion in the Hellenistic era of astrology. Those are the oldest versions extant, and they are the versions used in this book. As far as we can tell they reflect the earliest practice.

Ptolemy, the author of Tetrabiblos, has his own set of the terms, which he says was a correction on his part. However, by now it is pretty much recognized that Ptolemy himself was not a practicing astrologer, and does not reflect the typical practice of his time. Ptolemy's Tetrabiblos was enormously influential in the West, so you see his system of the triplicity and term rulers used by late Renaissance astrologers like William Lilly and John Gadbury, William Ramesey and other contemporaries. Modern followers of Lilly use his system.

So, be aware that if you look at the work of William Lilly, or of astrologers influenced by him, you will likely see some variation in the attribution of triplicity and term from what we are using here.

Rulership and the Thema Mundi

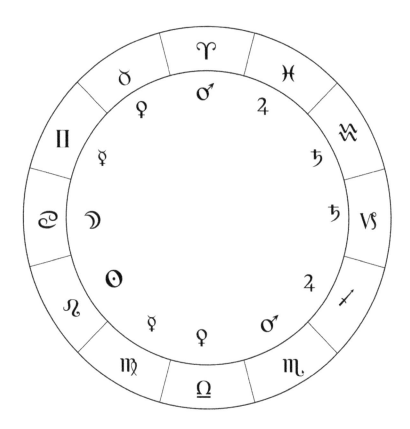

Figure 6: Thema Mundi Showing Sign Rulerships

The most important level of planetary position and responsibility, that of rulership, is determined in the logical and symmetrical order displayed in the diagram of the Thema Mundi shown here. The two Lights, the Sun and Moon, are given rulership over the two first months of summer, the time of the greatest light. The other planets are ordered in increasing distance from the two Lights.

Table 7: The Major Dignities

Planet	Rulership	Detriment	Exaltation	Fall
Sun	Leo	Aquarius	Aries	Libra
Moon	Cancer	Capricorn	Taurus	Scorpio
Mercury	Gemini, Virgo	Sagittarius, Pisces	Virgo	Pisces
Venus	Taurus, Libra	Scorpio, Aries	Pisces	Virgo
Mars	Aries, Scorpio	Libra, Taurus	Capricorn	Cancer
Jupiter	Sagittarius, Pisces	Gemini, Virgo	Cancer	Capricorn
Saturn	Capricorn, Aquarius	Cancer, Leo	Libra	Aries

Domicile/Ruler vs. Detriment

The ruler or domicile lord of a sign has the main authority and management responsibility for the affairs governed by the house that sign is in.

Note: *In traditional texts, there is an ambiguity in how the word house is used. Sometimes it refers to what we call the houses in modern astrology, and sometimes it refers to the Zodiac sign regardless of house placement. Domicile is another word for house or home, so Aries is said to be the house of Mars. I will stay with the modern usage to avoid confusion.*

Rulership is anabolic - it builds up, and acts in a relaxed and balanced fashion. A planet in its rulership is like someone safe in their own home, who knows where everything is. For a planet in its rulership things will tend to come together, and work out well. There will be a sense of confidence, control, unity, and competency.

The sign opposite that which a planet rules is where the planet is in detriment. Detriment is catabolic - things tend to fall apart, not work well. A planet in detriment will be off-balance, nervous, not at ease, not at home. There will be a sense of disunity, disorganization, corruption, incompetency to the action of the planet.

Exaltation vs. Fall

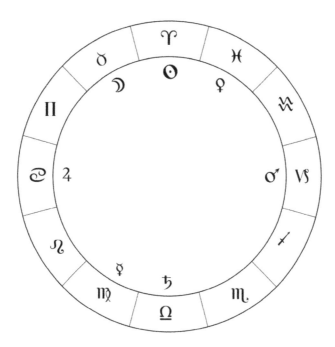

Figure 7: Exaltations of the Planets

Some scholars think that the dignity of exaltation may come from what was an alternate system of rulership. It is possible that our regular rulership attributions come from Babylonia and the system of exaltation from Egypt. Regardless of its source, the exaltations of the planets do not have the simple and symmetrical sense of order that we saw with rulership.

This diagram has the signs in the same location as the Thema Mundi, with Cancer, the sign of the Summer Solstice, over in the East in the position of the first house.

The dignity of exaltation is a measure of respect, recognition, honor, attention. An exalted planet is listened to, visible, of high value.

By contrast, a planet in the house opposite its rulership is in fall. This is the Rodney Dangerfield of dignities, in which the planet is not heard, not seen, ("I don't get no respect"), despised, of low value. Being in fall has some similarities to being in the 12th house.

Planets in fall often work hard to be heard or seen since they have the sense that no-one is paying any attention, and the planet will often act in an unbalanced way to try and compensate.

In the earliest texts, fall was strongly emphasized in importance, much more so than detriment.

The Minor Dignities

Note: *The addition of the 3 minor dignities adds quite a bit of complexity to the system. It is worth getting thoroughly comfortable working with the two major dignities and their debilities before you tackle the minor. Most of the examples later in this book concentrate heavily on the main dignities and their corresponding debilities, rulership, detriment, exaltation and fall.*

Most modern astrologers are familiar with the two major dignities that we have covered so far, those of rulership and of exaltation. There are another three levels of dignity used in traditional astrology, which are called the minor dignities.

When I talk about using the minor dignities in the following sections, if I sound tentative it's because I am. I think we have largely lost the meanings of these other dignities, and we are just barely starting to recover them in practice. Both the triplicity and the term rulers were widely used in the Hellenistic and Arabic periods, and each had its own distinct function. By the time of William Lilly, the different dignities had lost their specific flavor, and were just measures of strength and were assigned point values. For example, triplicity worth 3 points was defined as being weaker than exaltation at 4 points, but stronger than term at 2 points.

I've explored enough with triplicity and term that I am starting to get a sense of their distinct flavor, and I try to share that here. I don't yet have a handle on using face other than as a last-ditch way to avoid being peregrine. Think of the following sections as being an invitation to the task of recovering how these minor dignities can be used.

Triplicity or Trigon

The first, and I think the most important of the minor dignities is called triplicity or trigon. Trigon means trine, and the members of each triplicity, one for each of the four elements, are in a trine relationship with each other.

A triplicity is like an overall team, and each triplicity is assigned three different rulers, one for a day chart, one for a night chart, and a third planet called the participating ruler

Table 8: Triplicity Rulers

	day	night	Participating
fire	Sun	Jupiter	Saturn
air	Saturn	Mercury	Jupiter
earth	Venus	Moon	Mars
water	Venus	Mars	Moon

To understand the traditional triplicity attributions you need to remember how the planets are divided by sect.

The day planets are Sun, Jupiter, Saturn, and sometimes Mercury.

The night planets are Moon, Venus, Mars and sometimes Mercury.

The two active elements, fire and air, are considered diurnal, so they get the daytime planets as their triplicity rulers.

The passive elements water and earth are considered nocturnal, so they get the night planets as their triplicity rulers.

I think of the triplicity rulers as being like managing members of one or other of the two parties, night and day. Their influence seems to be less specific and more an indication of general good or bad fortune. This is not direct authority, but does enhance a planet's function. This connotes general, and not specific, good fortune.

A planet in its triplicity in a natal chart is more at home, more functional, more likely to act in a positive way. It doesn't have the same sort of direct authority as rulership or exaltation but's it is comfortable, it is *in its element.*

In Hellenistic astrology, all three of the the triplicity rulers of the sect light (Sun in a day chart, Moon in a night chart) are used as a general indicator of overall good or bad fortune for the native's entire life. Triplicity rulers of a particular sign or planet seem to have a similar significance for just that topic.

The triplicity rulers were heavily emphasized in Hellenistic and Arabic texts, but not used as much by the time of the Renaissance and later. The earlier texts used all three rulers, but by later periods, only the one main ruler of either the day or night was used, and the third participating planet was pretty much dropped. The earlier practice of using all three triplicity rulers was lost.

In natal interpretation, a planet having dignity by triplicity is more likely to be helpful in its effect. It does not have the major effect of rulership or exaltation, but it is positive.

When I do natal reading, following earlier, usage I use all three of the triplicity rulers, and give them about equal weight.

Bounds or Terms

The next minor dignity is referred to as term in most Renaissance era texts. The word bound is another translation, and means a confined or allotted area, which is closer to the meaning of the original concept. The word term also has that connotation when we speak of someone's term of office, meaning the confined period in which it starts and ends.

The terms divide each of the signs into five sections, one for each of the planets other than the two Lights. They are irregular, ranging from two to eight degrees in size. In general the planet with the first term has some other positive rulership in the sign, and the last of the terms is always assigned to one of the malefics, Mars or Saturn.

Table 9: Term Rulers

In the following table, the leftmost column shows the sign. The next columns, in pairs, show starting degree of the term, and the planet ruling that term.

♈	0	♃	6	♀	12	☿	20	♂	25	♄	30
♉	0	♀	8	☿	14	♃	22	♄	27	♂	30
♊	0	☿	6	♃	12	♀	17	♂	24	♄	30
♋	0	♂	7	♀	13	☿	18	♃	26	♄	30
♌	0	♃	6	♀	11	♄	18	☿	24	♂	30
♍	0	☿	7	♀	17	♃	21	♂	28	♄	30
♎	0	♄	6	☿	14	♃	21	♀	28	♂	30
♏	0	♂	7	♀	11	☿	19	♃	24	♄	30
♐	0	♃	12	♀	17	☿	21	♄	26	♂	30
♑	0	☿	7	♃	14	♀	22	♄	26	♂	30
♒	0	☿	7	♀	13	♃	20	♂	25	♄	30
♓	0	♀	12	♃	16	☿	19	♂	28	♄	30

Note: *You may ask, why are the Terms divided up the way they are; what is the logic? I'll tell you... I don't know... but it's a Tradition!*

There is no clear rationale that I am aware of for where each section begins and ends. Added up, the total number of degrees for each planet is a number associated with its planetary period. These term divisions go back to the earliest sources we have, without explanation. They seem to work.

The rulership level called bounds or terms seems to be a low-level or localized responsibility. If the exalted planet is the owner, and the ruler is manager, then triplicity is the management team, and the term lord is immediate supervisor. This is the level that dictates how things are actually carried out.

The dignity of term seems to affect the final earthing or manifesting of the matter. Any planet producing a concrete effect in a term has to go through the term ruler for its final expression

The term rulership seems to have been most heavily used with predictive techniques. For instance, there is a form of primary direction called distribution through bounds, which is used to find the time lord or ruling planet for a particular time period.

I have also used term rulership in fine-tuning interpretation, since it seems to color the final expression of the planet it rules. It seems to be more specific in meaning than triplicity. The better I know a person, the more I can see the effect of the term ruler on any given planet's expression.

Face

Face is the most minor of the dignities. Each 30 degree sign is divided up into 10 degree segments called faces, which are the same divisions as what modern astrologers call the decanates, which is a Vedic or Indian system that has been imported to the West. The rulership of the faces is assigned in reverse planetary order, going from Saturn and working in towards the Moon, then repeating. The series starts with Mars ruling the first face of Aries, Sun the second face, Venus the third face, Mercury the first face of Taurus and so on. The whole series ends with Mars ruling the third and last face of Pisces.

Table 10: Face Rulers

Sign	0° - 9° 59'	10° - 19° 59'	20° - 29° 59'
Aries	Mars	Sun	Venus
Taurus	Mercury	Moon	Saturn
Gemini	Jupiter	Mars	Sun
Cancer	Venus	Mercury	Moon
Leo	Saturn	Jupiter	Mars
Virgo	Sun	Venus	Mercury
Libra	Moon	Saturn	Jupiter
Scorpio	Mars	Sun	Venus
Sagittarius	Mercury	Moon	Saturn
Capricorn	Jupiter	Mars	Sun
Aquarius	Venus	Mercury	Moon
Pisces	Saturn	Jupiter	Mars

The system of rulership by face may go back to an earlier Egyptian system. Its meaning has been mostly lost in the surviving traditional astrology, and is not used much. The classical astrologer Lee Lehman, following Lilly, associates it with fear or nervousness, being out-of-balance, just one step from being homeless and out in the street. Face is that last ditch bit of dignity that keeps a planet from being peregrine. Other than that I am not aware of its distinct function.

Note: *There is a book that was recently published by Austin Coppock on the faces, that explores their history and meaning in detail. I am not familiar with that work, but I want to mention it here.*

Other conditions related to dignity

Peregrine

If a planet is in a sign and degree where it has no essential dignity at any of the five levels, it is considered to be peregrine, which literally means wanderer. In this case, since a peregrine planet has no dignity of its own, it completely depends on the condition and placement of its ruler to function. It is homeless, and at the mercy of the good will and capability of its host.

Almuten

Since there are 5 levels of dignity, at a given degree different planets will have different levels of rulership, and sometimes a single planet can have multiple dignities at a given degree.

The planet with the most cumulative dignity at a given degree is referred to as the Almuten, which is derived from an Arabic term meaning victor.

In Arabic and later traditional astrology, the almuten was usually used with a weighted scoring system for the five dignities, in which ruler = 5 points, exalted=4, triplicity=3, term=2, face=1. At any given degree you add up the number of rulership points for each planet at all five levels of dignity, and the planet with the most points is the almuten. The almuten is not always the same as the sign ruler. While the ruler will always have a strong influence on a planet in its house, the planet which is almuten for a given degree will also have a strong influence.

Backup Plan

I coined this term since it is a procedure that I have seen repeatedly in traditional texts. In discussing how well a planet will perform, I have repeatedly seen the following sort of structure: If the ruler of a house or planet is in poor condition, check the exalted ruler. If that is in poor shape, then check the triplicity rulers, and so on down the line.

The idea seems to be that a planet in good condition at a lower dignity can still contribute positively when a higher level ruler is in bad shape. The lower level ruler can be a backup. If dad is sick or injured, then the eldest son can help out. If the manager is out of action then a supervisor can step in.

I use this technique of the backup plan, and it works really well. It can be used in natal chart interpretation to look for effective options in how to deal with problem points. If you have a planet whose ruler is in poor condition, you would check the exalted ruler to see if that could be helpful. If the exalted ruler is in bad shape, you could then look at the three triplicity rulers, and so on down the line, looking for a planet in good condition that could be a positive influence at that location.

In the interpretation part of this book, you will see how the backup plan is a way of seeing where in a chart a debilitated planet could expect to be assisted by other planets.

Note: *On the following page is a pair of tables that summarizes all of the five levels of essential dignity.*

Table 11: Summary of Essential Dignities

Table of Dignities

Sign	Ruler	Detriment	Exaltation	Fall	Triplicity			Face		
					Day	Night	Partner	0-10	11-20	21-30
♈	♂	♀	☉	♄	☉	♃	♄	♂	☉	♀
♉	♀	♂	☽		♀	☽	♂	☿	☽	♄
♊	☿	♃			♄	☿	♃	♃	♂	☉
♋	☽	♄	♃	♂	♀	♂	☽	♀	☿	☽
♌	☉	♄			☉	♃	♄	♄	♃	♂
♍	☿	♃	☿	♀	♀	☽	♂	☉	♀	☿
♎	♀	♂	♄	☉	♄	☿	♃	☽	♄	♃
♏	♂	♀		☽	♀	♂	☽	♂	☉	♀
♐	♃	☿			☉	♃	♄	☿	☽	♄
♑	♄	☽	♂	♃	♀	☽	♂	♃	♂	☉
♒	♄	☉			♄	☿	♃	♀	☿	☽
♓	♃	☿	♀	☿	♀	♂	☽	♄	♃	♂

Term or Bound Rulers

♈	0	♃	6	♀	12	☿	20	♂	25	♄	30
♉	0	♀	8	☿	14	♃	22	♄	27	♂	30
♊	0	☿	6	♃	12	♀	17	♂	24	♄	30
♋	0	♂	7	♀	13	☿	18	♃	26	♄	30
♌	0	♃	6	♀	11	♄	18	☿	24	♂	30
♍	0	☿	7	♀	17	♃	21	♂	28	♄	30
♎	0	♄	6	☿	14	♃	21	♀	28	♂	30
♏	0	♂	7	♀	11	☿	19	♃	24	♄	30
♐	0	♃	12	♀	17	☿	21	♄	26	♂	30
♑	0	☿	7	♃	14	♀	22	♄	26	♂	30
♒	0	☿	7	♀	13	♃	20	♂	25	♄	30
♓	0	♀	12	♃	16	☿	19	♂	28	♄	30

Chapter Fifteen:
Modes and Angularity

We have one more important set of concepts that we need to cover before we can talk about the Planets, Signs and Houses. These are the concepts of mode and of angularity.

I am covering the modes and angularity together because they parallel each other and are both related to the symbolism of the number 3. The number 3 moving through time gives us a 3 stage process, with active beginning, sustaining middle, and changeable and transforming end.

In the astrology cycles, moving through time, you will see two different versions of a 3 stage process - cardinal/ fixed/ mutable in the signs, angular/ succedent/ cadent in the houses.

Take the 3 stages and combine them with the 4 elements and you get the 12 signs of the Zodiac. This takes the elements and makes them each part of a larger process.

Modes

Table 12: Zodiac Signs by Mode

	cardinal	fixed	mutable
fire	Aries	Leo	Sagittarius
water	Cancer	Scorpio	Pisces
air	Libra	Aquarius	Gemini
earth	Capricorn	Taurus	Virgo

The modes are all measured through time. They are phases of a life process of growth and decline.

The three modes are cardinal, fixed, and mutable, also called movable, fixed, and common.

These phases correspond to 3 phases or months of each of the 4 seasons - so, there is a cycle of 3 within a larger cycle of 4.

Cardinal, also called **movable** - initiates, starts, changes.

Fixed - continues, stabilizes, and gives form.

Mutable, also called **double-bodied** - has aspects of the other two - flexible, going back and forth, unstable, ready to change but not initiating the new, responsive.

The modes seem to be weighted more heavily than the elements in traditional interpretation.

For instance, one of the first things to look at when interpreting a chart is the Ascendant and the Midheaven, which are the two main angles of the chart, and determine their mode. - Their mode probably indicates a primary way the person acts in the world. I have found that to be a powerful interpretive principle.

In terms of the strength of their action, the cardinal signs come on the strongest. The fixed signs are less immediately strong but more sustained. In terms of external action the mutable weakest and most internal. The mutable signs are also associated with mental work or internal processing.

Angularity

The two main angles of an astrology chart are the Ascendant/Descendant axis, and the Midheaven / Immum Coeli axis. The angularity or strength of planet is measured by how close to one of the angles the planet is located.

The three qualities of angularity are

Angular, or close to an angle, or in the first house near the angles, the first, fourth, seventh and tenth houses.

Succedent, in the house or section succeeding or after the angle, the second, fifth, eighth and eleventh houses.

Cadent, which literally means falling away, in the house furthest away from the previous angle but not yet close to the next angle, the third, sixth, ninth and twelfth houses.

Remember that the daily motion of the Sun and the other planets through the sky goes in clockwise order through the chart, in opposite order of the houses. Think of a planet approaching an angle as getting gradually stronger, peaking when it reaches the angle, then rapidly falling away in effectiveness and power as it moves past the angle and recedes. In its daily motion, the Sun gets stronger as it goes through the 11th house, reaches its peak in the 10th house, and then rapidly declines and begins its downward movement in the 9th house.

Angular connotes strength, a start, rapid growth, initiation, visible action in the world.

Succedent tends to maintain, flourish, sustain, conserve, and hang onto. Succedent is the most stable of the 3 kinds of angularity.

Cadent connotes a transition, breakdown, instability, or a harvest. Cadent also is associated with awareness, mental processing as a kind of fruit before the husks are discarded.

The angularity of a planet is a measure of the strength or activity of the planet in the world.

Planets near the angles will be the most active, the most visible, and the most involved in the world.

Planets that are succedent are not as strong and visible as angular planets, but still considered effective.

Planets in the cadent houses will be less active, less effective in outer action, weaker, more hidden. However, you can also understand planets in cadent houses as having their greatest effect either internally, or in terms of consciousness.

The active planets by the angles get things done; the cadent planets withdraw, meditate, think about it, learn lessons, and become more conscious. The cadent houses are, in a sense, between the worlds.

Angularity is not a measure of the quality of how a planet acts. It is a measure of its *visibility, power and effectiveness* to take action in the world. When we discuss dignity in a later chapter, you will see that a planet can be right on an angle and very strong, but be in bad shape. That means any negative effect it has would be strong and visible.

Section Three: Planets, Signs, Houses

Chapter Sixteen:
Planets

I am going to build much of the basic interpretations of the planets, and the planets in their signs, from the building block characteristics. The purpose of this is to teach how to think in terms of the basic qualities. For example, if Mars is described as extremely hot and dry, what does that mean in the context of chart interpretation?

However, take into account that the planets are a kind of irreducible starting point, a set of symbols that cannot be explained just from their elemental characteristics.

Consider the following metaphor for understanding the planets.

The planets can be considered living beings - calling the planets gods is coming close - more like lower level, non-absolute gods, close to what the Christian cosmos would have called Archangels. The planets mediated the will of the supreme god(s) of the Primum Mobile, or highest divine realm, to the sublunary world of the elements, the earth.

So, the planets have personality, power, and authority - they act like autonomous beings that are are not just 'inside us' or under our control. Each of the planets has its own sphere of responsibility and influence, a limited or delineated power. And, like other living beings, a planet can be in good or bad shape, strong or weak, in a good or bad mood.

To paraphrase Aleister Crowley - whether or not the planets are gods or living beings really doesn't matter - the point is, the universe behaves as if they are, so it is a useful metaphor for thinking about the planets in astrology.

Always keep in mind *the basic concept of the planets having responsibility or rulership over different aspects of experience*.

Each planet is playing its part in executing the order of the cosmos in our sublunary sphere of the elements.

Much of the descriptive language of traditional astrology is very concrete, and talks about specific people, places, and qualities. Along with saying that Saturn represents age or fear or limitation, we say that Saturn rules old people, cemeteries, the skeleton, ruins, dark abandoned places, arthritis, and so on. Notice that the language is rich and concrete rather than abstract, and you draw the overall feel and action of a planet from those images.

General notes

The diurnal planets, Sun, Jupiter and Saturn are more conscious and visible, more public. By contrast, the nocturnal planets, Moon, Venus and Mars, are more feeling based, not as accessible to conscious thought, and often more private.

In terms of their elemental makeup, both malefics are dry, both benefics are moist. Both malefics are extreme and unbalanced, both benefics are moderate and balanced.

Warm Jupiter is a warm diurnal planet, cool Venus is a cool nocturnal planet. The benefics are in the sect that matches their nature.

It is the opposite with the two malefic planets. Hot, dry Mars is balanced by being in the cool nocturnal sect. Cold dry Saturn is balanced by being in the warm diurnal sect.

The planets in astrology do not have a single, simple meaning. It is worth remembering that the planets, or signs, or any other of the elements of astrology, take their meaning from the context of the question that is being asked of the chart. For example, depending on your question, the Moon could signify your emotions, your body and health, your stomach, your mother, milk and white foods, the common people in an election, and so on.

In traditional texts, descriptions of the planets are lists of the kind of things, places, situations, events and so on that the planet was said to rule. Our whole modern notion of reducing a planet's meaning down to a main keyword or concept is really foreign to how astrology was conceived.

Notes on the Planets

Note: *I will discuss the major dignities and debilities of the planets in the chapter on the signs, so they will be only briefly mentioned here.*

Sun - moderately hot and dry, diurnal, masculine and life-giving. The Sun can be malefic and excessively hot. If a planet gets too close to the Sun it is called combust, literally meaning scorched or burnt.

The Sun is vitality, life energy.

It is also prominence, visibility, authority. Depending where it is, it can mean how much prominence and visibility the native has, or who has authority over them, or sometimes both in different areas.

And, of course, the Sun is royalty.

The Sun is masculine, and can stand for men in general, the father, the husband.

In modern astrology the Sun is the key to the person, but in traditional, it not nearly so heavily emphasized, and the Sun is not considered as the key to a person's real identity. So, a traditional astrologer would never say that someone 'IS' a Gemini or a Pisces based on the sign position of their Sun.

In traditional astrology, the Sun shows vitality and prominence; it can show where you want those qualities - where you 'want to shine' - or, it can show areas of life people have authority over you. Depending on location the Sun is not always you - it can be your father, your husband, your boss.

The condition of the Sun is also an indicator of overall health, vitality, energy.

The Sun rules Leo, is in detriment in Aquarius, and is exalted in Aries and in fall in Libra.

Being hot and dry, the Sun has analogy by elemental balance to the 3 fire signs, in which the Sun also has dignity by triplicity. Other than its signs of detriment and fall, the Sun seems least happy in the the cold, wet water signs since you have conflicting elemental qualities.

Moon - cool and moist - the wettest planet, the most nocturnal, and the most feminine.

The Moon is reflective, dependent. It rules the night, which is the most inner focused and least outwardly visible period of the day. This is the opposite of the Sun's outward shining activity.

It is also the most feminine planet, and rules women in general, the mother, the wife, thus also nurturing, nursing, caring, tending, protecting.

The Moon is also considered changeable, unstable. It moves most rapidly and changes in appearance more quickly and extremely than any other planet.

In mundane astrology the Moon signifies the common people.

The Moon rules Cancer, is in detriment in Capricorn, is exalted in Taurus, and in fall in Scorpio.

The Moon has dignity by triplicity in all of the water and earth signs. The cold wet Moon gets along best with the cold, wet water signs with the exception of Scorpio in which it is in its fall. I suspect its unhappiness in Scorpio is partly related to the sign being so fixed and internal, and partly due to the rulership of hot dry Mars. With the earth signs, the Moon is happiest in her exaltation in Taurus, the wettest of the earth signs in a wet season, and least happy in very dry Capricorn, ruled by Saturn.

The Moon has antipathy by element to the hot and dry fire signs, and seems to be less sensitive and receptive there.

Mercury

The element attributed to Mercury varies according to its sign and any planets closely aspecting it.

Mercury is associated with consciousness - it is a bridge or a divider, a mediator, a messenger, and the interface or meeting place of differences.

Mercury is usually associated with what we call conscious thought - analyze, interpret, explain.

Mercury can also be a trickster, a 'devil's advocate', fault finder, a deceiver, and a juggler.

Since Mercury is interchange (s)he rules commerce, and money as medium of exchange.

Mercury can also signify what our internal communication is like, how intellect and feelings interact. Being many-sided, Mercury can be turned inwards toward the dream world, or outwards towards the objective world.

Mercury is the most elusive planet to pin down in meaning - elusiveness is one of the associations of Mercury! - and yet it is one of the most crucial to chart interpretation since it is the conscious mediator between opposites - inner and outer, night and day, diurnal and nocturnal, and so on.

Mercury rules Gemini, and both rules and is exalted in Virgo. Mercury has his/her detriment in Sagittarius, and is in both detriment and fall in Pisces.

Mercury has dignity by triplicity in all of the air signs, and is also generally at home in the air element since it has analogy with thought and communication. Some modern astrologers give Mercury exaltation in Aquarius.

Venus, the lesser benefic, is moderately cool and moist, feminine, nocturnal.

Venus relates or binds things together.

She is beauty, aesthetics, the arts, balance, and good proportion.

Venus rules clothing as adornment, cosmetics, jewelry - actresses, models, courtesans, artists, performers, dancers.

Venus is cooking for aesthetics and pleasure, as an art form and for balance - cooking for nourishment would be the Moon.

Along with the Moon, Venus is feminine, and rules all women.

She is friendship, love, good will, attraction, a force that harmonizes and brings together. As Mercury could be Truth, Venus is Beauty.

Venus rules Taurus and Libra, is in detriment in Scorpio and Aries, and is exalted in Pisces and in fall in Virgo.

Venus has dignity by triplicity in the two nocturnal and receptive elements, water and earth. Being predominantly cool and moist, Venus seems least happy by element in the hot and dry fire signs, where her cool receptivity has least affinity.

Mars, the lesser malefic, is excessively hot and dry, nocturnal, but the only masculine nocturnal planet. Recall that malefic Mars is grouped with the cool moist nocturnal planets, which moderates some of his hot, dry, extreme quality.

Mars cuts, burns, divides, and pierces. It is hot, extreme energy.

Mars is also anger, hostility, aggression, assertion, drive.

In positive ways, he can be energy, self-assertion, courage, hard work.

Mars rules soldiers, conflict, armies.

He also rules hot diseases - rashes, fevers, wounds, eruptions.

Since Mars rules cutting, he expresses in swords, knives, butchers, carvers, surgeons.

Mars is also related to fire - blacksmiths, wood burners, and welders. The plant tobacco is sacred to Mars, and is a plant which is burned and smoked.

As we mentioned earlier, note that the nocturnal planets tend to be more emotion based and hard for the conscious mind to get a handle on. The day planets are more visible, more direct to our waking minds.

Note that Mars the malefic is hot, and the night is cool. It is nocturnal because the cool of the night balances the excessive heat of Mars.

My experience is that Mars is a hard energy to control because it is not conscious, thoughtful, receptive or self-aware. There is something primal or archaic about this beastie!

Mars rules Aries and Scorpio, is in detriment in Libra and Taurus, and is exalted in Capricorn and in fall in Cancer.

Hot and dry Mars has affinity with the hot dry fire signs, so the effect of Mars can be strong even in the fire signs in which he has no dignity.

Being nocturnal, Mars has dignity by triplicity in the water and earth signs. However, hot dry Mars has elemental antipathy with the cold wet water signs, so his action there is somewhat problematic, even in Scorpio which is ruled by Mars. Even with dignity by triplicity, Mars in Cancer is both in fall and in a cold wet sign, so Mars is very unhappy there; dignity by triplicity does not outweigh the negative effects of fall and of the elemental mismatch.

Jupiter, the greater benefic, is moderately warm and moist. He expands, grows, enhances, gives life and has some similarities to the Sun.

Jupiter rules religion, spirituality, and aspiration, ideals, philosophy, and also law, authority.

Among occupations Jupiter rules priests, lawyers, professors, philosophers, astrologers.

In balance Jupiter is abundant growth; out of balance, there can be problems with excess.

Jupiter rules Sagittarius and Pisces, is in detriment in Gemini and Virgo, and is exalted in Cancer and in fall in Capricorn.

Jupiter has dignity by triplicity in the nocturnal fire and air signs. The warmth of those signs suits Jupiter's warm diurnal nature. Being warm and moist, Jupiter also has elemental affinity with the air signs, although that does not keep Jupiter from being unhappy in Gemini where he is in detriment.

Saturn. The greater malefic, is excessively cold and dry. Saturn blocks, divides, terminates, shrinks, chills, and is associated with obstacles, difficulty, fear, aversion.

In another way Saturn is associated with anything to do with Time - form, growth, decay and death, the Grim Reaper when Time runs out.

Saturn crystallizes, gives final form, defines, limits, divides, and differentiates. Saturn's energy is cold, objective, distant.

Along with time Saturn is also age, and the wisdom of age, old things in general, including the study of old subjects. Thus, traditional astrology could be considered to be ruled by Saturn since it is a study of an ancient subject, and traditional astrology tends to be more stoic and severe like Saturn.

Saturn is associated with old people, cemeteries, cold dark places like cellars and caves, old houses, old authorities, also old and rigid rules.

Saturn rules Capricorn and Aquarius, is in detriment in Cancer and Leo, and is exalted in Libra and in fall in Aries.

Saturn has dignity by triplicity in the diurnal signs of the elements fire and air. However, cold dry Saturn also has an elemental mismatch with the hot and dry fire signs, and is in debility in two out of three of them, Aries and Leo. Cold dry Saturn has elemental affinity with the cold dry earth signs, but Saturn is malefic and unbalanced so this is not always a good thing.

The Lunar Nodes

The two Nodes of the Moon are traditionally called Caput Draconis and Cauda Draconis, or the Dragon's Head and Dragon's Tail. They are the two points where the orbit of the Moon crosses the Ecliptic, the orbit of the Sun. Whenever a Full Moon or New Moon takes place close to one of the Nodes, there is an eclipse.

The word Node is from the Latin word meaning knot, and the Nodes are the place where the orbits of the Sun and Moon cross and are knotted together.

The North Node is where the orbit of the Moon crosses to go above or North of the Ecliptic. The South Node is the inverse.

These two points were imagined as the head and tail of a dragon, and since they are eclipse points they are places where either the Sun or Moon gets swallowed up by the dragon.

In traditional astrology the North Node is considered to be of the nature of Jupiter, and it increases or enlarges the power and activity of any planet in close proximity. Think of the North Node as a place where energy is increased and pours in.

The South Node is of the nature of Saturn, and it decreases and weakens the power of any planet in close proximity. Think of the South Node as a place where energy is decreased and pours out.

I use only conjunctions when looking at the effect of the Nodes, and I pay attention when planets are in the same house as one of the Nodes regardless of orb. They seem to have an effect in an entire sign. I weigh the effect of the Nodes increasingly heavily when there is an aspect of around 8 degrees or less.

The Outer Planets

I will not go into detail on the meaning of the modern outer planets, Uranus, Neptune and Pluto. When first approaching traditional astrology, it is both important and helpful to work with just the traditional planets, the Sacred Seven that are visible to the naked eye.

Since the addition of the outer Big Three, a lot of what were meanings of the main 7 were split off and given to the new planets. So, for instance, Spirituality goes to Neptune instead of Jupiter, and Death goes to Pluto instead of Saturn.

This has led to a thinning and loss of the complexity of meaning of the main seven. Disciplining yourself to work with just the seven allows you to rediscover more of the multivalent richness of their signification.

I do use the outer planets in my own work, but I always start interpreting a chart by casting it only with the traditional sacred seven. I do the first full cycle of interpretation on that part. This gives me the structure, the skeleton, the main outline of the chart, and much of the main meaning.

On the second pass through the chart I add in the outer 3 modern planets. However, I will give those planets emphasis only if they are in a tight degree aspect to one of the Sacred Seven, and they seem to be particularly important if they have a tight aspect to one of the inner personal planets, Sun, Moon, Mercury or Venus.

I often see charts that make much more sense and have a richer meaning with the outer planets added than without them. In the interpretation section I will include the outer planets on one of the charts, that of the philosopher Friedrich Nietzsche, in which I think a lot of the meaning of the chart is lost without them.

I always pay consistent attention to the outer planets in transits. They also seem to be of major importance in mundane astrology that spans long periods of time and affects masses of people.

Chapter Seventeen:
The Signs

Introduction

The Sun, the Moon and the other wandering planets, move in their daily path around the earth, and in a yearly path through the backdrop of the fixed stars. The Sun's path defines a circle around the earth that we call the ecliptic.

The 360 degree circle of the ecliptic is divided up into twelve equal 30 degree segments that are the Signs of the Zodiac.

The Signs in Traditional Astrology

Signs in traditional astrology are not emphasized anywhere near as much as in modern astrology.

Modern astrology is very sign-based, so much so that we say that someone "IS" a Pisces, or "IS" a Taurus, based just on location of their Sun at birth.

Traditional astrology emphasizes the planets, and the houses, quite a bit more than the signs. The signs basically serve as an environment or setting that determines how well a planet will be able to function. This is largely a function of the dignity, or condition, that a planet has in a given sign.

Signs by themselves do nothing. They are an environment for the action of the planets.

The planets are primary, the source of all action. The sign a planet is in serves as an environment for how the planet expresses. The house is the area of life the planet operates in. So, with traditional interpretation we start with the planet and not the sign.

The Signs and the Basic Building Blocks

In the following descriptions of the basic nature of the signs, we are going to build their meaning from the ground up, using the building blocks we discussed in the chapter on the basic concepts - the 2 sects of day and night, the 2 genders, the 4 elements, the 4 seasons, and the 3 modes of action.

In the following, remember the meanings of the modes -

Cardinal - action, initiation, change, moving quickly

Fixed - sustained, structured

Mutable - flexible, wavering, also more self-reflective

And, the meanings of the elements -

Fire - action, passion, external directed

Earth - structure, stability, practicality

Air - dispersion, intellect, connection, communication

Water - emotion, reflection, passivity, sensitivity, internal

Other Associations

Much of the meaning of the signs is derived from the meaning of the planets with major dignity in the signs, rulership and exaltation. So we will mention the planets that have dignity in each sign, and how that relates to the sign's meaning.

If you read traditional texts, you will see that, along with the building blocks of the elements and modes, the signs have other attributions such as parts of the human body, different kinds of terrain, different animals, and so on. The signs are described in terms of concretes and specifics rather than general concepts.

Descriptions of signs

Aries - cardinal, fire, masculine, spring season. Hot and dry at new beginning season of year. Cardinal, which means quick acting but not sustained. Good at starting but not continuing. Aries is fire so planets here are active, and not necessarily thoughtful or reflective. Aries is not a sign that is generally sensitive to others.

The ruler of Aries is hot, fiery Mars, and the hot, fiery Sun is exalted here. All of the energy of Aries is fast-moving, outgoing, active, initiating things. This also means that the sign is not receptive, not reflective or self-aware. It is the start (cardinal) of the warm (fire) season of the year.

Sensitive, receptive, moist Venus is in her detriment here. There is nothing receptive in this sign for Venus to work with.

Cold, dry Saturn is in his fall here. The cold stasis of Saturn and the hot movement of Aries are opposites, so Saturn is in a bad mood in this sign.

The symbol is the Ram's head.

Taurus - fixed, earth, feminine, spring - a cold dry element in a warm moist season - I think of this as like the moist and fertile Spring soil at the time plants are really starting to grow from the increasing warmth of the season. Sustained, stable earth plus fixed mode emphasizes its heaviness, stability, dependability, passivity, and stubbornness.

Warm and moist, receptive Venus is in her rulership here, and adds her moisture to make the earth fertile. Cold and moist Moon is exalted here.

Hot, fiery Mars is in his detriment here, and is about as effective as a sword cutting through thick spring mud.

The symbol of Taurus is the Bull.

Gemini - mutable, air, masculine, spring - mutable air in the spring or air (warm and moist) season, so air scattered in all directions. Air doesn't get any airier than this.

Mercury is ruler - very strong and 'in his element' but not necessarily most useful or practical. Mercury likes to connect with others in this air element, but being mutable it can fly off in all directions.

Jupiter is in detriment - Jupiter is most effective with expanding structure, and Jupiter scatters rather than expands here.

The symbol of Gemini is the Twins.

Note *that all of the mutable signs are described as double-bodied, which matches the back and forth, unstable, wavering quality of the sign. There also seems to be a self-reflective, inward, mental quality to all of the mutable signs.*

Cancer - cardinal, water, feminine, summer - water that is warm, moving, outgoing, so it has an active, nurturing quality. This is the first sign of the season of summer, when growth really kicks into overdrive.

This sign is a cold, wet element in the hot, dry season of summer, so there are some contradictory qualities here. Cancer can be outgoing and nurturing, but also withdrawing and protective. The cardinal quality of Cancer works with the hot quality of the season to make this the most initiating and moving of the water signs. Cancer is rushing water, streams at full strength moving swiftly.

Moon, the Mommy planet, rules here, and the Moon is the source of most of the meanings we associate with this sign - nurturing, maternal, protective, family oriented. This is an extremely fertile time of year.

Note that the two Lights, the Sun and the Moon, are given to the first two months of summer when there is the most light.

Jupiter is exalted in Cancer - Jupiter's expansive magnanimous quality is given a sensitive, nurturing quality from the moving water.

Saturn is in his detriment - Saturn blocks the water's flow, and is cold and dry in a summer sign. Also, since the Moon (along with the Sun) is one of the planets that are considered for physical health and vitality, Saturn in Cancer can mean a block or restriction on physical health and energy.

Mars is in his fall - Hot dry Mars and all that water don't mix. In general, a planet in its fall is ignored, not heard, not respected. You have the self-assertive Mars in a sign oriented towards nurturing others, so Mars can get cranky here.

The symbol of Cancer is the crab.

Leo - fixed, fire, masculine, summer. This is a hot and dry sign in a hot and dry season, so it comes on very strong. Leo is a fixed sign which is sustained more than Aries, so it stays very strong. This is the peak of the summer - fixed, dry, relentless, steady, unending heat.

The Sun is the ruler of this sign, and is hotter and stronger here than anywhere else. This is also the sign in which the Sun is the most visible and prominent.

Saturn is in detriment here. You have the hottest and brightest of signs and the coldest and darkest of planets. However, Saturn is dry as is fire, and Leo is also fixed, so you can get a negative sort of rigidity here. There is no flexibility or receptivity here, just a rigid clash of opposites.

The symbol is the lion, king of the beasts.

Virgo - mutable, earth, feminine, summer. Virgo falls at the beginning of the harvest season. This is a mutable sign, a transition, in which summer is starting to fall apart and you sense the first signs of approaching autumn. Change is in the air, and things are not stable. Like other mutable signs, Virgo has a self-reflective quality - you can think of it as an inner equivalent of separating out the wheat from the chaff during harvest.

Mercury is in both rulership and exaltation. This is Mercury in a dry earth sign which gives the planet some structure and substance to work with. Mercury can be more detailed, practical, and useful here than in Mercury Overdrive Gemini, which can get scattered.

Jupiter is in detriment here. Jupiter thrives where it can expand and build, and here structures are being taken down, dissected, harvested, and broken apart. The two energies work at cross purposes. If Jupiter is associated with faith then Virgo is critical self-doubt.

The symbol of Virgo is the Virgin, often pictured as a woman holding a sheaf of wheat associated with the harvest.

Libra - cardinal, air, masculine, autumn. This is the first of the two seasons where cold dominates, and where the night is longer than the day, the beginning of the decline of the Sun. This is the peak of harvest time, and also the season when the leaves in temperate climates turn their brightest and most brilliant before they fade and fall off the trees.

Venus is the ruler of this sign. This is sensitive, receptive Venus in a warm and moist air sign, and I think this is where we associate most of the meaning of Libra as has having to do with relationship, communication, and awareness of the needs of other people. That is Venus combined with air. Also, Libra is cardinal which makes Venus more outgoing in initiating friendships.

Saturn is exalted here. Saturn has an association with judgment and discrimination, which is where we get the Libra association of fairness to others. The warmth and connecting moistness of the air in a day sign tempers some of Saturn's cold, dry quality, and brings out the best in this planet.

The combined attributes of Venus and Saturn give us most of the usual associations for the sign Libra - Saturn provides objectivity and fairness in judgment, Venus provides the empathy for others.

Mars is in detriment here. Mars is a hot, outgoing planet in a cold and dry season of the year, in a moist receptive sign. Mars is a primitive and selfish energy, and that is a poor match for this sign's environment. Mars in Libra is like Sylvester Stallone being cast for the lead in Mary Poppins - a poor match at best, irritable and unable to perform well.

The Sun is in fall here, in the time of year when its powers of light and heat are starting to decline and the night is longer than the day. Also the Sun is all about shining (Notice Me!), and Libra is about relationships and others.

The symbol of Libra is the Scales, which suggests weighing, balancing, accepting and rejecting.

Scorpio - fixed, water, feminine, autumn. This is a cold wet sign in a cold dry season. Scorpio is the 'driest' of the water signs, partly from being fixed, partly from the season associated with cold, dry earth.

The season is cold and dry, the sign is cold, wet and fixed. This is the time of year when the leaves are brown and fallen, the trees are bare, and the nights are getting longer. With all that cold and fixed energy being emphasized, this sign is more internal, less outgoing. Also, an inner movement is shown in the withdrawing of life from seasonal plants, being drawn down inward and into the earth as leaves are shed, plants die, turn brown, wither and start to decay.

Its ruler is hot, fiery Mars, which is strong here but not particularly active. Mars gives this sign its reputation for intensity - think hot, glowing, fixed, buried fire, like volcanic lava trapped below ground under pressure, or like frozen fire beneath a layer of ice.

Venus is in her detriment here. The cold and dry of the season, and the fixed quality of the sign, work against Venus and her receptivity. The water can give it sensitivity, but it is one that is not easily expressed, especially with Mars ruling the show here. Venus is most expressive when outgoing, and the energy of this sign is very much turned inward.

The symbol of Scorpio is of course the Scorpion, which emphasizes the notion of the attack energy of Mars turned inward.

Sagittarius - mutable, fire, masculine, autumn. This is the most mutable, reflective, and intellectual of the fire signs. Late autumn is not a time for active physical striving, so here fire expresses as aspiration, ideals, and striving to attain those ideals.

The meaning of Sagittarius is largely colored by Jupiter being the ruler of this sign. There is an association with law, philosophy, benevolent optimism, striving after ideals. Jupiter has a mental quality - mix that with fire, and you get much of the meaning of Sagittarius.

The symbol for Sagittarius is the Archer and the Centaur, half man, half beast. This is another of the double-bodied, mutable signs. It has a reputation for being either idealistic or sensually self-indulgent, depending on whether the man or the beast is dominant at the moment.

Mercury is in his detriment here. Idealistic, system building Sagittarius, colored by Jupiter who rules the sign, is not a place where Mercury's emphasis on detail and definition in communication can easily express. Here you get some of the negative associations of Mercury, as trickster, liar, undependable, deceiving.

Capricorn - cardinal, earth, feminine, winter - cardinal plus earth makes for sustained action - cardinal starts it, earth can keep going once in motion

Here is a case where you have to think in terms of planet taking priority over sign.

If you look at modern astrology books on the signs, you will often see Capricorn described as ambitious, hard-working, and needing to conquer and achieve in the world.

Sun Capricorn is often described as being ambitious in acting in the world. I think that is as much a quality of Sun (ambition, prominence, fire) as it is of Capricorn. That is very much a function of Sun-in-Capricorn rather than Capricorn by itself.

I often read descriptions of Capricorn on the Ascendant as having similar qualities to Sun in Capricorn. The British astrologer Charles Carter pointed out that is often not the case, and Capricorn rising people are often more reserved and private, less ambitious and active. Take the Sun out of the equation and emphasize the ruler Saturn more strongly and that makes perfect sense. The sign Capricorn by itself does nothing, but colors the action of planets within that sign.

As we have seen repeatedly, ***the sign takes its color and meaning largely from the planets that have dignity here***.

Again, signs by themselves do nothing. Planets act in signs, and the planet is primary. With, Capricorn, the modern meaning of the Sun in this sign has overly colored our understanding of the sign itself.

Saturn is the ruler of Capricorn. Saturn is cold, dry, reserved, and practical, in a cold winter sign. I think this emphasizes what can be the shyness and reserve associated with this sign. Saturn is not particularly outgoing or ambitious, so Capricorn can be cautious, guarded, practical but not necessarily striving for worldly accomplishment.

Mars is exalted in Capricorn, which I think is another place that we get our association with Capricorn as being ambitious, hard-working, and striving.

The Moon is in her detriment here. You have the cold wet Moon in a cold dry element in the coldest season of the year, ruled by cold dry Saturn. This is not a good place for the Moon to be empathizing, nurturing, sympathizing and helping growth. Never mind feelings, we have practical work to attend to!

Jupiter is in fall here. Capricorn is far too cold and dry for warm, moist Jupiter to feel at home. Saturn's rulership here just doesn't listen to Jupiter.

Planets in Capricorn often have a dry, practical, reserved, matter of fact quality to their expression. Remember, Saturn rules here!

The symbol of Capricorn is the Goat. Some older texts give this sign a monstrous beast that is half goat and half fish.

Aquarius - fixed, air, masculine, winter - this is a warm moist sign, in a cold moist season, but fixed. Air is intellect, but the fixity adds stubbornness.

Much of the modern meaning of the sign Aquarius is derived from its association with Uranus as its modern ruler. That is where we get the notion of Aquarius as the lone rebel and crusader for change.

In traditional astrology Aquarius is ruled by Saturn. If there is idealism (air) to this sign it also has rigidity, a lack of receptivity or flexibility. People devoted to an ideal can be very intolerant of those who do not share that ideal, and I think that is related to the sign being ruled by Saturn. Also, Saturn adds to the impersonal and group-oriented flavor of this sign. I think of Charlie Brown saying, "I love humanity, it's people I can't stand". This is not so much an individualistic, uranian idealism as it is an impersonal, collectively oriented, Saturnian sort of objectivity.

The Sun is in his detriment here. This is the dead of winter, a cold and impersonal, Saturn ruled sign, so the Sun's light and heat is very weak.

The sign of Aquarius is the water-Bearer, a man bearing an urn of water being poured out.

Pisces - mutable, water, feminine, winter - a cold wet sign in a cold wet season - it is mutable, so it has no fixity or structure. This is the most watery of the water signs - hard to pin down, flexible, receptive, emotional. It doesn't get any wetter than this. If Cancer is a cardinal running river and Scorpio is fixed ice, then Pisces is the mutable ocean - universal, moving outward in all directions, emphasizing the lack of boundaries often associated with this sign. Also, as with other mutable signs, there is an introspective, self-conscious, inward-turned reflective quality to this sign.

Pisces is very colored by the season - that unstable time when winter is breaking up but spring isn't quite here. Also, this is typically a wet time of year - you get melting snow depending on your climate, you can get late winter or Spring rains or snow - and, with the melting, you get the rotting remnants of last year's leaves and plants which have been sitting under a snow pack for the Winter, or otherwise lying idle.

Jupiter is the traditional ruler of Pisces. Jupiter's empathy and compassion combine with the mutable receptive quality of water to give a kind of universal, unselfish compassion at best. However, Jupiter's expansiveness combines with Pisces ultra-wet, mutable lack of boundaries to sometimes give excess, which can express as self-indulgence, or an overly self-giving martyrdom.

The spiritual side of Pisces is often associated with its modern ruler, Neptune, but traditionally Jupiter is associated with religion and spirituality. The modern planet Neptune's meaning is already contained in the symbolism of the traditional ruling planet Jupiter.

Mercury is in his detriment and fall here. With all this abundance of wet, Mercury expressing here is like trying to write on water.

The symbol of Pisces is the pair of fishes swimming in opposite directions. Slippery!

Chapter Eighteen:
The Houses

Before we start interpreting the meaning of the houses, please recall that traditional astrology views the house structure as a completely independent system in its own right. It is important to make the mental effort to set aside the modern notion of sign and house meanings being the same.

Even though I agree that there are some parallels in meaning between signs and houses, approaching them as different systems will allow you to see more of the nuances in meaning of each independent of the other.

My own opinion is that the meanings of the houses are neither completely parallel to the signs, nor are they completely separate. The truth seems to be somewhere in between, in which there are some striking parallels in meaning but some significant differences also.

The houses and the signs appear to have different origins, with the signs most likely coming from Babylonian astrology and the houses coming from Egyptian roots.

The Zodiac is universal. At any given time, from the earth, all of the planets occupy exactly the same position by sign and degree. However, *the house system is personal*, since it is measured from the native's particular location at a specific point on the earth.

If I look out in all directions around me, I see the circle of the horizon, with the bowl of the Zodiac rotating in a roughly east to west direction. The part of the Zodiac that is coming up over the horizon on the east is the Ascendant, and the point opposite that is the Descendant. The highest point that the Sun reaches above me in its travel is the Midheaven, and below me is the IC or Immum Coeli, bottom of the heaven.

Starting at the Ascendant, the wheel of the Zodiac is divided up into twelve sections relative to where the native is, and those twelve sections are the Houses.

The Houses show how the universal Zodiac is related to my personal situation in my unique life on earth.

Quadrant Houses

There are different ways of dividing up this space around the native into twelve sections, and they are referred to as **House Systems.**

In quadrant systems the Ascendant is the cusp or beginning point of the first house, and the Midheaven is the cusp of the 10th house. They are called quadrant because the 4 points, Ascendant, Midheaven, Descendant and IC divide the circle up into 4 sections or quadrants. The different kinds of quadrant systems have different rules for dividing up each quadrant into three sections or houses.

Because those 4 points (ASC, DSC, MC, IC) are relative to the the rotation of the earth on its equator, and the ecliptic (apparent path of the Sun and the Zodiac) is at an angle to the equator, the position of those points and their relation varies according to season of year. The latitude (distance north or south of the equator) of the observer, the difference between Ascendant and Midheaven is often not exactly 90 degrees in Zodiac longitude. So, the houses are not all the same size in degrees on the ecliptic.

The effect gets more pronounced at higher latitudes. In extreme cases you can also get intercepted signs, in which all of a single Zodiac sign are within the boundaries of a single house without that sign being on either cusp.

The most commonly used house system is **Placidus**, largely because Placidus tables of houses were widely available and common in the 1800's thanks to Raphael's Ephemeris. Basically, Placidus is the most common system today because most people use it.

For many astrologers, the preferred house system will vary depending on your teacher, or on what astrologers you have read. For example, many people who are strongly influenced by William Lilly use the Regiomontanus system because that is the one Lilly used. Regiomontanus is very popular in England. Some traditional astrologers favor the Alchabitius semi-arc system because it is one of the oldest widely used quadrant house systems. Similarly, many astrologers in England use what are called Equal Houses, because prominent British astrologer Charles E O Carter favored that system.

Whole Sign Houses

The main house system that I use in this book is called **Whole Sign Houses**, and it is the earliest house system that we know of, going back at least to Hellenistic Astrology prior to the first century AD. Whole sign houses are also used in Vedic astrology, and have been in the entire history of that branch of astrology.

With Whole Sign houses, the entire first house is the entire sign that the Ascendant is in. The boundaries of the houses and the boundaries of the signs coincide. This means that the Ascendant can be anywhere in the first house, and any planet in the same sign is considered first house whether it is above or below the Ascendant.

The Midheaven in Whole Sign houses is not the cusp of the 10th house. In fact, it can be in the 9th, the 11th, or sometimes even the 8th or 12th house depending on latitude or time of year. The Midheaven still does relate to reputation and visibility in the world. If it falls in a different house, that can color its meaning. For example, a Midheaven falling in the 9th by Whole Sign could indicate a career involving education, religion, law or travel.

Trying Out Whole Sign Houses

I encourage you to experiment with Whole Sign houses as you familiarize yourself with the astrology interpretation rules in this book. Try drawing up charts you know with this house system also, and see if they provide any additional information.

If you do try changing house systems from what you are used to, be aware that moving from quadrant to Whole Sign house systems can feel like an identity crisis ("what do you mean, Saturn isn't in the 9th house anymore?"). Some people can take some time to comfortably make the switch, or to consider a different house system from the one you find most familiar. In your own chart you can be very comfortably used to the location of planets in particular houses and what that means, and often, with Whole Sign houses, the house positions of planets can change. This will change how your chart reads, and making that change can be difficult.

It took me personally around a year and a half from when I first started playing with Whole Sign Houses to when I dove in and made the switch to Whole Sign as my primary house system. Now that I am used to reading with Whole Signs, it feels utterly natural. For a few years I used only Whole Sign Houses; currently I use both Whole Sign and Placidus for different information.

With Whole Sign houses, some of the interpretive techniques covered in this book will be easier to see and understand.

If you use quadrant houses with the techniques in this book, I encourage you to print out your chart with proportional rather than equal house sizes so that you can more clearly see the signs and angles.

Using Multiple House Systems

I think it is worth trying out Whole Sign houses, not to replace the house system you currently use, but as an alternate, a second system that provides another point of view.

Even though I use Whole Sign Houses in the examples in this book, I have had experiences where I needed to use both Whole sign and Quadrant house charts to do a complete reading. Both systems work, from different angles, and they can provide different and complementary information.

In one of the examples later in the book, I will look at the chart with both Whole Sign and Placidus houses, and you will see that both charts work, and in that particular example, both charts were needed.

There are also interpretive situations like intercepted houses that occur in Quadrant but not Whole sign houses, which can be meaningful also.

There is historical precedent for using multiple house systems like this. Ben Dykes has pointed out that the Arabic astrologers Sahl and Masha'Allah used both Whole Sign and Quadrant house systems.

I now use Whole Sign as my primary house system, but I also check Placidus houses to see how the planetary placement shifts between them. I consider them both valid and sometimes compare them, laying them next to each other and looking at both at once.

General Notes on the Houses

The houses are divided up into benefic or favorable, and malefic or unfavorable. The division depends mainly on whether or not they can see or aspect the Ascendant. In the following figure, note that houses 6,8, and 12, which are the three houses considered malefic, are all are averse to the Ascendant. House 2 is also averse the Ascendant, but it is not usually given a negative connotation. As the house that immediately follows the Ascendant, the 2nd house supports it. We associate it with belongings and wealth; in a related way, it can also be the second or stand-in in a duel, or someone in a helper or assistant role.

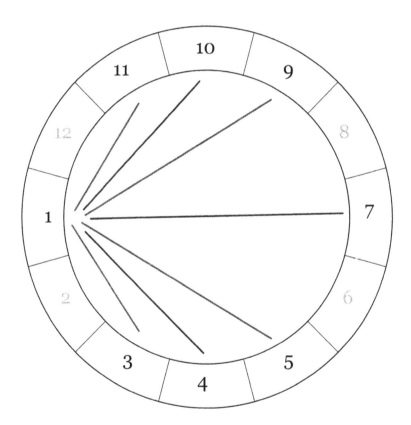

Figure 8: Thema Mundi Showing Aspects and Aversion

Houses are divided up in terms of strength, visibility and activity, according to how close the house is to an angle, moving counterclockwise with the signs. This is the division into angular,

succedent, and cadent, where the angular houses are considered strong
and the cadent houses weak.

The interpretive structure that we call the the stakes, signs in a 90 degree
cross with each other, is related to the concept of angularity. From any
given point in the chart, those planets that were in signs angular to that
planet were the strongest and most active.

The houses are also divided up by elevation, where planets that are in
houses above the horizon are sometimes considered stronger than those
below because they are visible. Often, the most elevated planet in the
chart, the planet closes to the top of the chart around the 10th house, will
be particularly important. Correspondingly, a planet down in the 4th
house can be hidden or private.

A planet's strength varies according to which house the planet is in, with
some houses considered more powerful or outwardly effective than
others. The relative strength of the houses is in this order -

1, 10, 7, 4   - the 4 angular houses
11, 5, 9, 3   - not angular, but aspect the Ascendant
2, 8, 6, 12   - the 4 houses averse from the Ascendant

The four angular houses, starting with the first and tenth houses, come
first.

The next two houses eleven and five , are succedent houses that aspect
the Ascendant by Whole Sign. Houses nine and three are cadent but
aspect the Ascendant.

The last four houses are the ones that have no Whole Sign aspect to the
Ascendant. They are considered disconnected, out of awareness or
averse. House two, which relates to money and belongings, is the only
one that has a positive connotation.

The other three are the houses that are considered malefic or unfortunate,
houses eight, six and twelve, in order of increasing misfortune.

Flexible House Systems

Many of the older traditional texts also seem to have a more flexible sense of house systems. Houses did not always start from Ascendant, but were also used with the first house starting at a point or planet being examined. Most notably, it was common to count houses from the location of the Lot of Fortune for general fortune - but there were also houses of the location of the Sun and for the other planets, for special purposes.

Derived Houses

Traditional astrology also uses what are called derived houses, where a house's meaning is taken from its distance from another house that sets its subject. For instance, in traditional astrology the 10th house is associated with the mother because it is the 7th house (house of marriage partner) from the 4th house of the Father, and lineages were determined from the male. Similarly, the eighth house refers to your partner's money since it is the second (money) house from seventh (partner).

Traditional vs. Modern House Interpretation

In modern astrology the entire chart is largely viewed as psychological and in your head and the entire chart represents you. By contrast, in traditional astrology, you are the first house, and the other houses are other aspects of your life and environment, many of them external to you and out of your control. So, for instance, the tenth house is not your attitude to your career, but could be the career itself, or could be other people in a position of authority over you. The seventh house is not how you relate to your partner, but is the partner him or herself.

I think that, in using traditional astrology interpretation, both the character analysis and external description meanings of the houses seem to work. The two dimensions complement each other. In traditional interpretation any descriptions of a house's meaning would stay close to verifiable aspects of the person's outer reality.

Note that the various meanings of a given house are not necessarily related - the houses have different meanings for different subjects and in different contexts. For instance, the 6th house has meanings related to small animals, illness, your work or your servants, and, in mundane astrology members of the armed forces. This does not mean that small animals owned by soldiers who work for you are connected to making you sick.

I will be covering both modern and traditional meanings for the houses. You will see that some modern meanings fit well in the traditional astrology framework, and some do not.

Following this chapter there is a summary table of the meanings of the Houses in traditional and modern astrology.

The Houses in Pairs

The pairs of houses that are opposite each other have related meanings, and often a planet in one house will affect the theme of the opposite. So, we will cover the houses by pairs to show the connections.

I will begin with the most prominent and powerful houses, since planets in them will often dominate the chart. These are what are referred to as the angular houses.

Angular Houses

The First and Seventh Houses
The Ascendant and the Descendant
The Self and the Other

First House

The first house stands for you, or the native. It shows your personality, your appearance to world, your style of communicating, character, and physical appearance.

The Ascendant, and the first house, is YOU, and the rest of the chart is the world you inhabit and interact with.

To interpret the meaning of the first house, look at the sign, and the mode of the sign the Ascendant is in. Also, look at any planets in the first house, and at the ruler of the first, its location and tradition. All of these factors affect interpretation personality, characteristics, and manners.

The first house is associated with Mercury as communicator and mediator, since the Ascendant is where the native communicates with the rest of the world. It is Mercury's house of Joy.

Seventh

The seventh house signifies anyone opposite. This could be either your partner or spouse, or an opponent or enemy.

These are people or parties that are visible, known to you, with whom you have a one on one relationship.

In business deals it is either your equal partner, or your competitor and enemy. In sports astrology it is the other team. In war, it is the enemy country, and so on.

Planets in the seventh house usually stand for other people or parties. Often, even in a psychological interpretation, the native does not recognize the qualities of the seventh house as belonging to them, but sees them in other people.

The Fourth and Tenth Houses
(The Midheaven and Immum Coeli, or MC and IC)
Public World and Private World

Tenth

In most house systems the Midheaven defines the start of the tenth house. The Midheaven is where the path of the Sun, Ecliptic, reaches its highest point of elevation in the day's journey. The opposite point is called the Immum Coeli or bottom of the heavens. They are usually abbreviated MC and IC.

The tenth house is related to your occupation, reputation, and your career, not necessarily how you make money but how you are viewed in the world. It is the most publicly visible and prominent of the houses.

The tenth house is also those in authority over you - your boss at work, or someone who has public power in your life.

From another point of view the tenth house can be your goal, your ideal, what you strive for, what you wish to achieve.

The tenth is also associated with the mother, since it is the seventh or partner house from the 4th house of the father. When I am looking for family or ancestors in general I use the fourth house, but if I am specifically interested in the mother as the father's wife I use the tenth house.

Note that there is not necessarily any connection between the tenth house being related to the Mother, and the tenth house's connection to career and reputation. The connection of tenth house with the public parent and the 4th house with the at-home parent is very much a modern notion.

The tenth house is out in the world, visible, public.

Fourth

The fourth house is associated with ancestors and family. In a culture that measures lineage through male parents, this is primarily the father.

The fourth house is also your home, land, the base you come from, the past. It is the foundation of your life.

In horary astrology the fourth house is the end of the matter, and in the cycle of life the fourth house is related to the end of your life, the circumstances of your death.

The fourth house, being at the bottom of the chart, is private, hidden from the world, personal.

--

With the other, non-angular houses, we will go around the circle in order.

Second and Eighth Houses

Second

The second house is possessions and assets rather than values, so it has a narrower, more specific meaning than in modern astrology. The word value is a vague and all-inclusive term. A person's values are found all over the chart. For instance, a planet in the seventh house could show what a person values in a relationship. As in much of traditional astrology, it is worth staying close to the concrete, physically verifiable meaning.

The second house is also whatever is close to you, what supports you. In a duel it is your second, in a contest it might be your partner.

Eighth

This is one of the three malefic or unfortunate houses. If you look at the Thema Mundi diagram, you will see that there is no whole-sign aspect between the first and the eighth houses. Planets in the 8th house are out of touch, out of control, sometimes out of consciousness.

The eighth house is the house of death. Not transformation, but death.

I think that some modern astrologers use the word transformation to skip over the negative connotations of death and move straight to positive after-effects or rebirth. That is not how the house is viewed in traditional astrology. Yes, there can be a rebirth or transformation when encountering death, but that does not make it any less death.

The fourth house is also your partner's assets, since it is second from seventh. It can also have to deal with handling other people's money, so a stock broker might have a strong 8th house.

In traditional astrology the fourth house no connection to sex. That is very much a mid-20th century innovation.

The fourth house is also associated with anxiety, fear, phobia, panic. There is a sense of a passivity that is unable to act. That is related to the house being averse from the Ascendant, so planets here are have difficulty finding expression. In some traditional material you will see the fourth house described as idle, which is related to that same inability to act.

And finally, the fourth house can have a connection to the occult, probably as related to the dead. This could be spiritualism or necromancy, dealing with the realm of the dead,.

Third and Ninth Houses

I want to start by looking at these houses as a pair. In traditional astrology the ninth and third are the two houses related to religion, spirituality and philosophy. The ninth is the house of God and is related to the Sun, and the third is the house of the Goddess, and related to the Moon.

Both these houses have themes of spirituality and religion, in which the ninth is public and third is private and personal religion. Or, the ninth could be the religion in favor, while the 3rd is out of favor.

The ninth can be the official outward religion, and the third can be any kind of alternate or opposing spirituality or religion - the third is also the house of heresy.

The ninth/third axis can also be public/private spirituality.

As cadent houses, the pair are related to ideas, awareness, internal processing.

So, the meanings of these two houses are quite a bit richer and more intertwined in traditional astrology than in modern.

In traditional astrology it does not make sense to assign religion to the ninth house and spirituality to the twelfth house. To a traditional society it would be meaningless to separate the two.

Apart from spirituality, the third and ninth houses also have their own meanings as follows.

Third

The third house is related to siblings, close neighbors, those parts of your family and neighborhood who are your peers. The third and fourth houses together are related to home, family and upbringing.

The third can also be related to communication, writing, commerce, and short journeys.

In the area of education, the third house can stand for lower or mundane schooling like grade school. With the third/ninth house polarity, it could be an alternate or non-official style education.

The third house is the Moon's house of Joy.

Ninth

As in modern astrology, the ninth house is related to religion, law, higher education, major travel, teaching, and publishing. In education it covers college or graduate level, and can be related to continuing education in general.

The state of this house often shows a lot about values related to education, ethics and religion, how important they are to the native, and how they will be approached.

On a larger level the ninth house is related to religion, the church, philosophy and laws.

Fifth and Eleventh Houses

These two houses are both consistently viewed as benefic or positive, and are associated with Jupiter and Venus.

These two, along with the second and the eighth, which are at right angles to the fifth and eleventh, are sometimes referred to as the substance houses, and these four houses together show a lot about the financial well-being of the native.

Fifth

The fifth house in traditional astrology is primarily the house of children. It shows how likely it is that the native will have children, and can show something about what the children are like, or what the relationship with children will be like.

The fifth house is also recreation, enjoyment and pleasure, including sexual pleasure.

The fifth house as signifying creativity seems to be a modern meaning, although it does seem to work well, and is consonant with the other meanings of this house. If you connect it with the traditional meanings, it could be creativity that you do for pleasure or recreation.

The fifth house is also related to gambling and games of chance. Strictly speaking, investment in the stock market falls in the fifth house since it is a gamble, a game of chance.

It also can be related to love for fun, where you're in love and don't yet have a relationship with the beloved. Edgar Allen Poe, who had no children, has a very strong Venus in the fifth house, which is probably related to his poetry and his love and worship of one particular woman. That is a case in which the relation between the fifth house and creativity seems to work.

Eleventh

The eleventh is the house of good fortune. This can be as pennies from heaven, or money from those in authority since it is the second from tenth. It signifies hopes and dreams, and the fulfillment of those dreams.

The eleventh house is also often related to groups and communities of friends. These are clubs are groups you join because you want to. Eleventh house relationships are not as intimate as seventh house, direct one-on-one encounters. Planets in this house can signify the kind of people you hang out with, or people you meet in the groups you are part of. It can be communities of people with shared values.

The Sixth and Twelfth Houses

These two houses are the most consistently malefic or unfavorably interpreted houses. They are associated with Mars and Saturn, and both houses are averse to the Ascendant, so they are areas of life outside of the native's control.

There is not as much emphasis on ideas and awareness as with the third/ninth house axis. Here cadent means less visible to the world - activity that goes on behind the scenes, or the hard work in the background that goes unnoticed.

Sixth

The sixth house is not the house of health but of health challenges, problems, and illness - or rather, how vulnerable you are to health problems. A planet in the 6th in good condition can mean you tend to stay healthy and fight off illness. General health or physical well-being is shown by the first house which stands for the body.

The sixth house is related to work, but this is not the kind of work you do that brings you recognition. Traditionally the sixth is the house of your slaves, so the work you do here is the hard, unglamorous, working for The Man, slave labor kind of work. This is the work you do because you have to in order to survive

The sixth house is related to service, but it is hard, thankless, unglamorous service with no visibility and little reward. Dorothy day, who was active in the Catholic labor movement and founded many houses to help care for the poor, is an example of a person with a strongly emphasized sixth house.

Since this house has connotations of both illness and service, it can also be related to work in health care or nursing.

The word service has a certain amount of spiritual glamour in modern astrology, and the sixth house does not have that connotation. This is down and dirty service.

And finally, in some contexts the sixth house stands for small animals, smaller than the kind of animals you can ride. Traditionally these would be animals that you raise either for work or for food. Modern astrology also puts pets in this house, and though that is inconsistent with the traditional meaning I have seen that meaning work.

Twelfth

The twelfth is the worst of the worst, the most malefic of all the houses. You will find very little positive about the twelfth house in most traditional texts.

The twelfth house is confinement, isolation, prison or detainment, and is also related to illness along with the sixth house.

This house is behind the scenes, and can stand for hidden enemies, or for self-undoing, ways out of your awareness that you are your own worst enemy.

Interpreting the twelfth house as related to spirituality is very much a modern development. An example of such a connection of the twelfth with spirituality is the chart of Thomas Merton, the Trappist monk, who has a very strong twelfth house. Yes that is spiritual , but Merton was a monk who has renounced the world and chosen a life that is essentially voluntary poverty and imprisonment. There is nothing glamorous about that spirituality. This is spirituality in retirement or confinement, not in the public eye, withdrawn, hidden.

There is also a self-negating or self-undoing quality to any twelfth house spirituality. I have seen a twelfth house emphasis in charts in which the person's spirituality has a strong monastic, ascetic or self-denying component.

When the twelfth house is active in predictive work in the context of cycles, it can mean a period of withdrawal, isolation or lack of activity at the end of one cycle before beginning another.

The Joys of the Houses

Just as there are planets that have rulership in signs, so each planet is said to have its joy in a specific house. It is possible that this association goes back to an alternate system of planetary rulership.

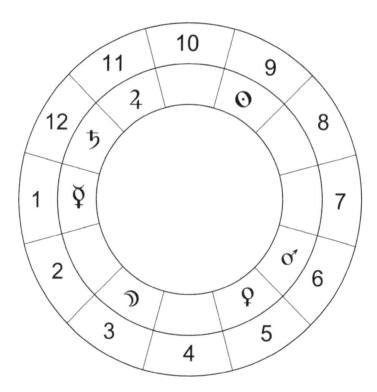

Figure 9: The Joys of the Planets

Here are the joys of the houses. They are in 3 pairs of polar opposites, with Mercury off by himself.

The eleventh house is Jupiter and the fifth house is Venus, so you have the two benefic planets associated with the two benefic houses.

The twelfth house is Saturn and the sixth house is Mars, so the two malefic planets rejoice in the two most malefic houses.

The ninth is the house of the Sun and of (masculine) God, and the third house is the Moon, or the house of the Goddess. In a modern setting, a strong third house could be related to Goddess or earth-based spirituality.

Mercury, the messenger and mediator has his joy in the first house, right on the Ascendant, so Mercury is on the border, the mediator. This is Mercury as consciousness itself, the interchange between day and night, above and below, consciousness that happens at the interface between opposites.

I think that all of these placements of the joys of the planets lend themselves to exploration through meditation.

Other Notes on the Joys

Here are other points to consider related to the joys of the planets.

All of the diurnal planets, Sun, Jupiter and Saturn, are above the horizon. All of the nocturnal planets, Moon, Venus and Mars, are below.

As we noted, the benefics Venus and Jupiter are in benefic houses, and the malefics Saturn and Mars are in malefic houses.

The two lights, Sun and Moon, are in houses associated with religion and worship, with the Sun God above the horizon and the Moon Goddess below, the Sun ruling the heavens above and the day, the Moon ruling the earth below and the night.

Mercury, which can be either diurnal or nocturnal, is on the Ascendant on the border between the two.

Note that the malefic planets' joys are in houses averse to the Ascendant, as if they want to hide their malice, lurking "in the dark" to create all kinds of mischief in the native's life.

The greater light's joy (Sun) forms a trine to the Ascendant while the lesser light's joy (Moon) forms a sextile. Sun's and Moon's joys are in challenging square relationships to both malefics' joys. The malefics' joys are in averse houses from the benefics and vice-versa.

The following two pages have a table that summarizes the meanings of the houses in traditional astrology, and how they differ from modern meanings.

Table 13: House Meanings in Traditional Astrology

	Attributes	Difference from Modern	Notes
1	Body, appearance, main character, temperament, personality, quality of mind, how one communicates.	Includes personality, character, and general health. In a sense, 'all' of the self is here.	Mercury affects meaning. No connection with Mars.
2	Money, small belongings. Material assets, livelihood, material fortune. Partners & associates (next to 1st)	Objects and money, not 'values'	No intrinsic connection with Venus.
3	Siblings, immediate neighbors and environment, day to day associates. Short journeys. Communication, writing, learning, religion and spirituality, education.	Related to 9th on spirituality and learning. May be earth/lunar religion rather than solar in 9th. Heresy as opposite 9th. Private rather than public spirituality.	Moon affects attributing learning, communication and short trips
4	Ancestors in general, father. Earth, land and property, house and residence. End of life, endings.	Ancestors in general. (10th is sometimes mother as 7th from 4th, spouse of father.)	Has analogy with meaning of Saturn, not with Moon.
5	Children. Pleasure, amusement, entertainment, the arts, sex. Gambling as amusement, games of chance.	Sex is here as pleasure.	Venus affects general meaning.
6	Health problems, illness. Nurses and health workers. Lack of recognition, unrewarding work. Slaves and servants. Small animals. Averse from Ascendant.	Health problems, not health. General health is 1st house. Work, but 'slave' labor, unglamorous service with no recognition.	Mars affects meaning. (In mundane, the army.)
7	One on one relationships. Marriage, partners, opponents, open enemies Other party in a business transaction or horary.		

House Meanings (continued)

	Attributes	Difference from Modern	Notes
8	Death, fear, anxiety, lack of control. Also called an 'idle' house. Spouse's money, legacies (2nd from 7th). Averse from Ascendant. Hard for planets here to be seen or act effectively. If 8th has an occult connotation, as necromancy, traffic with the world of the dead.	Sex in 5th, not 8th. Death and not 'transformation' or 'rebirth'.	
9	Long journeys, travel, foreign lands. Religion, spirituality, astrology, omens, dreams, divination. Learning and places thereof. Universities, churches.	No separation or opposition between religion, spirituality, mysticism, divination.	Sun affects meaning
10	Dignity, public reputation, fame, eminence. Most public house. Career as what you are known for. Superior or boss at work.	No particular connection with father.	Saturn NOT ruler, but very unfortunate here.
11	Friends, good fortune in general, money from superiors (2nd from 10th). Hope, trust, confidence.		Jupiter affects meaning
12	Hidden enemies, prison, confinement, self-undoing, illness, death. Large animals. Averse from Ascendant.	Not spirituality or mysticism, which are given to 9th/3rd axis. Possibly severe monastic isolation.	Saturn affects meaning, no analogy w Jupiter.

Angularity and Whole Sign Houses

The Whole Sign House system creates some interesting ambiguities when evaluating the strength of the planets, because the house divisions do not coincide with the angles.

With the Whole Sign house system, the Ascendant is always in the first house, but not at the beginning of it, and not even necessarily near the beginning of the first sign. It is perfectly possible to have a planet in the first house that is more than 10 degrees above the Ascendant.

The Midheaven in the Whole Sign system does not necessarily fall in the tenth house. You can have a planet in the tenth house that is not even in the same sign as the Midheaven, and could easily be more than 30 degrees distant.

So, how do you measure angularity and planetary strength? The source texts are ambiguous on that point since it is not always clear what house system is being used.

My interpretation of this issue is from the writings of Ben Dykes. He explores this issue extensively in the introductions to some of his translations.

Signs for Topics, Angles for Strength

Basically, the signs are used for the house divisions, and these determine subject areas of life.

Proximity to the angles, the ASC/DSc and MC/IC axes, determines the relative angularity or strength of the planets. If you take the distance between the horizontal and vertical axes in any quadrant, and divide it up roughly into 3 sections, any planet in the first section nearest the angle would be considered angular and strong; a planet in the second section would be moderately strong or succedent; and a planet in the third section would be considered cadent or weak.

The division I just described is the basis of quadrant house systems. Ben Dykes maintains that this quadrant division was originally used only to evaluate the strength of the planet and not for houses and topics.

Take a chart with the Ascendant at 20 Cancer, and Mercury at 5 Cancer.

Being in the same sign, Mercury is in the first house, and has first house meanings as relating to the personality, the sense of self, and the body and so on. However, since Mercury is 15 degrees prior to the Ascendant, it is weak in terms of angularity.

Ambiguity of Meaning

I find that having these two different divisions of the Zodiac circle mapped on top of each other, with one division signifying topics and the other signifying strength, creates some ambiguities in interpretation.

First of all, the terms angular, succedent and cadent now have two different meanings, one referring to topics, the other to strength. You can easily have a planet that is angular by house and cadent by strength. I think that blurs the meaning of these terms.

As an illustration, put the Midheaven in the eleventh House, which happens very often with Whole Sign houses. By topic this means that the person's Midheaven issues - visibility, prominence, action in the world - will have an eleventh house flavor - the person may be striving for prominence in groups they are part of, or among their circles of friends. That blends some tenth and eleventh house connotations together.

Now take that same eleventh House midheaven, and put a planet in the tenth house. The tenth house is in the stakes or at 90 degrees to the first house, so it is considered strong and influential in that sense. However, in terms of angularity measured from the Midheaven axis, the planet would be considered cadent or weak. So you can have a weak cadent planet in the tenth house of career and reputation.

Take again the previous example, with Mercury at 5 Cancer, the Ascendant at 20 cancer, and add Venus at 24 Cancer. Mercury is first house but cadent or weak, and Venus is both first house and angular/strong. Venus is the rising planet in this scenario even though it is not the earliest planet in the first house.

I wonder if there is any difference in how these planets are experienced by the native. Would Venus be more in their conscious awareness since it is below the Ascendant? Would Mercury be visibly first house to others, but not as conscious to the native since it is well above the horizon and thus cadent? It's like a planet well above the horizon in the first house takes on somewhat of a twelfth house flavor in the sense of being out of awareness, but not in the sense of hidden enemies, self-undoing and other twelfth house matters.

I have seen that kind of situation happen in a couple of readings I have participated in. Perhaps angularity also has something to do with conscious awareness along with being a measure of strength and ability to act.

I don't have an easy answer to these issues. I raise them here because I think they need to be tried in a lot more situations to get a clearer sense of how they act. The revival and widespread use of Whole Sign Houses in Western astrology is still relatively new, so I think we are still exploring the ramifications of this house system.

Chapter Nineteen:
Aspects

Geometry, Aspects, Seeing and Aversion

In traditional astrology aspects are based on the idea of planets being able to see each other, to be within each other's line of vision. The planets cast rays which enable them to see the other planets, and the angles of those rays correspond with what we call the Ptolemaic aspects.

This version of the Thema Mundi shows aspect lines from the Sun.

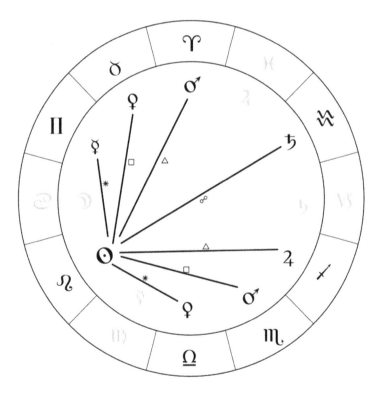

Figure 10: Thema Mundi, Aspects and Aversion

Starting from Leo, two signs away is sextile, three is square, four is trine, and six is opposition. In traditional terms this means that a planet in Leo can 'see' all of those signs.

The other signs, that are either one sign or five signs away and that are greyed out in the diagram, are not visible from Leo. They are referred to as averse, meaning turned away or not visible. The 30 and 150 degree signs don't see each other.

Thema Mundi and the Nature of the Aspects

We have seen how the different Ptolemaic aspects are derived from the angular distance of each planet's rulership from the Sun. The sextile is of the nature of Venus, the square of Mars, and so on. Each aspect has an affinity with the planet that defines it.

However, the affinity seems to work both ways. In his book on the Arabic Parts, Lind Weber notes that, according to Vedic astrology, planets have an affinity with certain aspects. Just as each aspect has an affinity with its defining planet, so each planet has an affinity with the aspect it defines.

For example, Jupiter would be most effective in a Trine relationship since it accords with Jupiter's nature.

So the Thema Mundi shows which aspect each planet 'prefers', which aspect is most effective or natural for that planet.

Given that geometric and planetary framework, we can explore how the aspects play out.

The Major or Ptolemaic Aspects

Conjunctions (0°) strictly speaking are not aspects - they are more like combinations or unions. I think you could say that a conjunction is more like one of the lights, the Sun or Moon - a matter of identity.

Oppositions (180°) are of the nature of Saturn - they oppose, block, hinder, fight, but they can also balance or complement, and can indicate relationship. Saturn, the lord of darkness and winter, is opposite the two lights that have their signs in the summer.

Trines (120°) are of the nature of Jupiter - harmonious, beneficent, smooth flowing, and working together.

Squares (90°) are of the nature of Mars - active, unstable, tense, irritable, stressful, demanding action.

Sextiles (60°) are of the nature of Venus - pleasant, amicable, cooperative, and relating. Sextiles are generally thought to be the weakest of the main aspects. Modern interpretation often says that sextiles take some work or communication to get a positive result, and that relates to the communication side of Venus.

The different aspects take on the quality of the number of the division of the circle - so the opposition is like the number 2, the trine like 3, square like 4, and sextile like 6, or 3 times two. The conjunction is like the number One, which is related to the Lights, i.e., a matter of union or identification.

The most important aspects are the conjunction, square, and opposition.

There is a lot of emphasis in traditional texts on what they refer to as the stakes - that cross shaped group of 4 signs in one of those relations with each other. In interpreting the condition of any planet or point, one of the first things you check for is other planets in the stakes from that sign. Those are the primary influences to evaluate.

Aspects are primarily by Whole Sign.

There are degree based aspects within an orb, but that is a kind of special, more intense subset of basic aspects by sign. Take into account that, with Whole Sign houses, the whole sign aspects cover the entire house the sign occupies.

Aspects, Seeing and Aversion

Aspects in traditional are all based on whether or not planets can see each other. The Ptolemaic aspects are the 'rays of vision' that a planet sends out that allows it to 'see' other planets. So there is a kind of geometry of vision at work here.

The angles that are not in a whole sign Ptolemaic aspect to each other are described as being averse, meaning turned away.

Planets , or houses, or signs, that are averse, do not see each other. They are out of touch.

Two of the modern minor aspects, the Semisextile (30°) and the Inconjunct (150°) are between signs that would be considered averse in traditional astrology. Even in the context of modern astrology, the inconjunct refers to a relation in which the two planets have nothing in common with each other and can't communicate. So in a sense, the inconjunct is an aspect that is of the nature of lack of aspect or aversion.

The planets aspecting or relating to each other, their nature and condition and how they combine, are more important than the specific type of aspect between them. It also seems that the existence of any kind of aspect between planets, even a stressful aspect, is more favorable for them than to be averse and out of touch.

It is indeed true that older texts refer to trines and sextiles as fortunate, and the squares and oppositions as seriously unfortunate. However, all the astrologers I know, whether modern or traditional, tend to reframe that, and interpret it as trines and sextiles being smooth and relaxed, squares and oppositions being challenging and intense. This is a case where most traditional astrologers I know have been influenced by the modern interpretation of those aspects.

Given that similarity, I think traditional astrologers are more likely to allow for the fact that a square or opposition between two planets in poor condition are likely to be unpleasant, unfortunate or threatening. Traditional astrologers seem more likely to allow for the fact that not all aspects can be controlled.

If a square or opposition is to turn out favorably, such a situation will likely take more work and be more challenging. But again, take into account that much of the effect of the aspect between planets depends on the nature of the two planets, the condition they are in, how those two planets naturally relate, and what kind of reception exists between them, a concept we will cover in detail.

An applying aspect is considered stronger than separating, and whether or not an aspect perfects is considered to be important. This is of primary importance in horary, but does not seem to be as strongly emphasized in natal astrology.

Aspects Have Direction

Aspects also have a direction. Between two points, the point that is earlier in Zodiacal order - moving counter-clockwise - is considered to be the planet having the primary influence. This is the planet that first rises over the Ascendant in its daily motion. An earlier planet in square to a later planet is described as overcoming the later planet it is aspecting.

So, for instance, if you take Mars in Scorpio square Venus in Aquarius, Mars overcomes Venus since it is earlier in Zodiac order. This aspect would be interpreted as Mars acting on Venus, and Venus receiving that action.

Take Jupiter in Pisces square Moon in Gemini. Jupiter overcomes the Moon ; in the repeating cycle of the Zodiac, Pisces precedes Gemini.

With Saturn in Libra trine Venus in Aquarius, Saturn is the earlier planet and is the dominant one in the aspect. You could say that Saturn aspects Venus, and Venus receives the aspect.

Whole Sign and Degree Based Aspects

In traditional astrology the primary relation between planets is by whole sign aspects. So, for example, any planet in Leo is in opposition by whole sign to any planet in Aquarius, regardless of how tight or loose the orb is by degree.

That basic relation of whole sign aspect always needs to be taken into account, especially with conjunction, square and opposition.

Aspects by degree orb can be considered as special cases of an intense and strong relationship. If you use the metaphor of sight with an aspect, if two planets are in whole sign aspect they are within each other's line of vision. If two planets are in degree based aspect they are staring at each other.

Many interpretive techniques for a planet look for the closest degree based aspect to that planet. That is looking for most intense focus of the planet's action.

Degree Aspects and Orb

In general, traditional astrology texts use more generous orbs than modern texts do. I suspect this goes back to aspects primarily being by whole sign, and only secondarily by tightness of degree.

In my own work, the orb I look at depends on the aspect.

I give conjunctions a wide 10 degree orb, or even more with the two lights, the Sun and Moon. The very fact that two planets are in the same sign (and the same house if you use Whole Sign houses) means that they will affect each other.

For oppositions and squares I use the same wide orb. I have seen planets in opposition by Whole Sign house that were more than 15 degrees out of orb but were obviously in an opposition relationship in the native's life. So, I think that whole sign aspects are primary and degree based aspects a special stronger case, especially when you are dealing with the stakes, planets in conjunction, opposition or square.

For planets in trine or especially sextile I think it is another matter. They tend to operate more in the background, and sextiles seem to be a lot weaker than any of the other traditional aspects. So, for a trine I will use up to around an 8 degree orb before I sit up and take notice, and for sextile I use maybe 4 or 5 degrees at maximum. For planets in these two aspects I don't think whole sign aspects are all that strong.

Out of Sign Aspects

An out of sign aspect is a relation between planets, in which they are in a tight aspect by degree, but where they are not in that same aspect by sign.

For example, Mars at 29 Pisces is trine to the Moon 28 Cancer - they are in trine aspect by whole sign and in trine aspect by degree. By contrast, Mars at 29 Pisces is averse to the Moon 2 Leo - they are within a trine aspect by degree, but are averse by whole sign aspect.

In traditional astrology as I have seen it practiced, only out of sign conjunctions are used. Mars at 29 Pisces is considered conjunct with Mercury at 2 Aries, even though they are not within the same sign. However, Mars at 29 Pisces is not trine Mercury at 1 Leo, even though they are within degree orb. The two signs are averse so there is no aspect in traditional astrology.

The primary aspect is the whole sign to whole sign aspect. Degree based aspects in traditional astrology are a special case within the category of whole sign aspect.

The signs for the most part are considered to be like discrete rooms or areas - the transition between them is understood to be sharp.

However, if you examine the medieval astrologer Guido Bonatti's 146 considerations, the most famous chapter in his massive Book of Astronomy, and some of the writings of Arabic astrologers, you will find that when a planet is in the last degree (29 degrees up through 29 deg 59) of a sign, it has lost all strength in that house, and all of its energy is in the house it is entering.

Similarly, a planet in the first degree (0 degrees through 0 deg 59) is not quite settled in its new sign. Those borderline degrees are considered weak and unstable. It is like a person standing in a doorway between rooms. I've found that planets in the last degree of the sign, while primarily in that sign, do take on some of the flavor or characteristics of the sign they are about to enter.

I think that is why out of sign conjunctions seem to work in traditional astrology. Using out of sign degree based aspects other than conjunction is a modern technique.

Interpreting Aspects in Context - Condition and Reception

When interpreting the effect of aspects between planets, the nature of the aspect itself is only one of the determining factors. Along with that, the quality of the expression of that aspect is influenced by many other factors, including
- the nature of the planets involved and their sympathy with each other
- any reception between them (to be covered later)
- the houses they are in
- general condition or dignity of the planets involved
- the type of the aspect itself - I put this factor last in importance.

Antiscia

Antiscia are sometimes called solstice points.

In a Zodiac circle, draw a line along the axis of 0 Cancer to 0 Capricorn - the axis of the two Solstice points. That is an axis of reflection, in which a point on one side of that axis, has a corresponding point on the other side that is exactly the same number of degrees from the end of the axis. That corresponding point is referred to as the Antiscia. The days on either side of the solstice point have the same amount of sunlight.

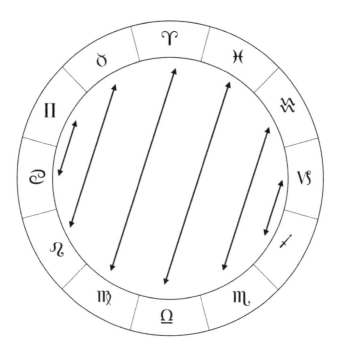

Figure 11: Antiscia

The signs on either side of the axis reflect to each other.

Cancer	to	Gemini.
Leo	to	Taurus.
Virgo	to	Aries.
Libra	to	Pisces,
Scorpio	to	Aquarius.
Sagittarius	to	Capricorn.

Once you know the corresponding sign, to find the antiscia of the point, take its degree position and subtract it from 30 degrees.

For instance, a planet at 17 Pisces has its antiscia at 13 Libra, and vice-versa. A point at 10 Cancer has its antiscia at 20 Gemini, and vice-versa. The relationship is always reciprocal. Once you know how to scan for them it is a pretty quick and easy process to pick them out.

Antiscia are also sometimes called, shadow points. When a planet is on the antiscia of another planet, the connection between them acts like a conjunction, but one that is in the shadows, hidden and surreptitious.

The orbs on antiscia are normally kept very tight, usually one degree.

The point that is directly opposite the antiscia of a planet is called a contra-antiscia. A planet on the contra-antiscia acts as if the planets were in opposition, but with the same shadow quality.

It is worth taking the time to scan for the antiscia of the planets in a chart, because they can show a powerful connection between planets that is not otherwise obvious. I find them to be consistently significant.

Chapter Twenty:
Reception

Reception is an important concept. Properly used, I think it is one of the keys to good chart interpretation.

To illustrate what reception means I want to start with an example. Let Mars be in Aquarius. Aquarius has Saturn as domicile lord or ruler. Aquarius is referred to as the domicile of Saturn, who is the lord, the head of the household. We say that Mars is received by Saturn into his domicile.

That is the definition of reception. Mars is in Saturn's sign of rulership, and Saturn receives him.

Mars is a guest in Saturn's household. Saturn, having responsibility for this sign or domicile, is obligated to see to the welfare of that sign, and the house it occupies, including the planets in it. So reception is a statement of the action of Saturn towards Mars.

You can have reception in the other dignities also. If Mercury is in Cancer, Mercury is received into the domicile or sign rulership of the Moon, into the exaltation of Jupiter, into the triplicity of Mars/Venus/Moon. Mercury would also be received by the term and face ruler he is in by degree, although they are not highly weighted.

Reception is an action or disposition of the ruler towards the ruled.

For reception to be useful, the ruler or Lord of the house has to have a whole sign aspect to the house ruled. With that aspect, there is a connection between the Lord and his or her house. Without that aspect - if the Lord is averse to the ruled house - then there is a lack of connection, and the reception is much less useful and favorable. Having the ruler averse would be like having an absentee landlord who did not leave a contact number; there is a lack of awareness and connection.

Mutual Reception

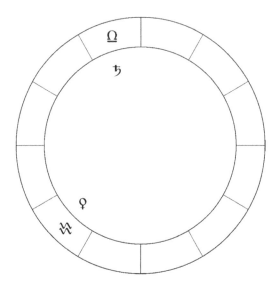

Figure 12: Mutual Reception

Let Venus be in Aquarius and Saturn be in Libra. Saturn receives Venus into his Domicile or Sign, Venus receives Saturn into her Domicile. Each occupies the sign that the other planet rules. This is called mutual reception by domicile or rulership. It is the most positive possible relationship between two planets. Each is favorably disposed towards the other planet, and they will act in mutually beneficial ways.

While mutual reception does have a positive effect on both planets, the dignity or condition of the planet in the sign and house where it resides still needs to take into account. In the above example with Venus and Saturn, Saturn in Libra has dignity by exaltation and triplicity, while Venus has no dignity in Aquarius. Thus, Saturn is likely to be the dominant planet in the relationship between the two. With the two in mutual reception there is likely to be a mutually beneficial relationship between the two planets, with the interaction being more strongly Saturn-flavored than Venus-flavored.

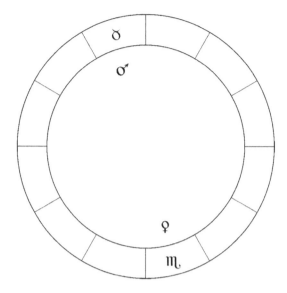

Figure 13: Negative Mutual Reception

By contrast, if Mars is in Taurus and Venus in Scorpio, the two planets have mutual reception by sign, but each planet is in its detriment, so neither planet is in particularly good shape. The planets have the responsibility to treat each other well, but can only act with the quality of the condition they are in. The mutual reception assists the two planets but does not erase each planet's debility.

The oldest texts say mutual reception requires an aspect between the planets. It is ambiguous as to whether this needs to be by degree or by sign.

Much of the earliest material interprets reception in the context of horary astrology, where whether or not aspects perfect, or come to an exact aspect degree relationship, determines the outcome of the question. In Horary it makes sense that reception would need a degree aspect to complete to be effective. Horary is used for prediction, and perfection of an aspect is necessary for an event to take place.

In natal work the completion of aspects seems to be less critical, so I think it reasonable to have whole sign aspects with reception The important point is that the two planets need to see each other by whole sign aspect. You can't really have a relationship unless there is some connection. If you are staying at my house as a guest, I can only treat you properly if I know you are there and we can communicate.

Some authors, notably Lilly and Gadbury from the early Renaissance period, use reception by itself without any mention of requiring an aspect. Some very skilled astrologers I personally know say that reception without aspect does have an effect. That is not strictly true to the traditional meaning of reception, but I respect conclusions drawn from chart reading experience. Even if you do allow reception without whole sign aspect, the state of aversion should greatly lessen how positive that effect is.

Mutual reception and Changing Places

Some modern astrologers say that having planets in mutual reception is equivalent to the two planets switching places so each is now in its rulership. So, with the Mars Taurus, Venus Scorpio example mentioned previously, mutual reception would make the two planets act like Venus in Taurus and Mars in Scorpio. That would effectively erase all debility.

This is a modern notion that I have seen credited to Ivy Goldstein-Jacobson, a skilled and witty astrologer who self-published many books in the last century.

Geoffrey Cornelius, in "The Moment of Astrology" (in 'Horary Revived - My Aunt's House' p 153) states that mutual reception in a horary can show a choice available to the querent, and switching the planets shows the results of that choice. He has a vivid and striking narrative of an actual horary using the switch to resolve a situation. In that situation it takes a deliberate action with intent by the native to activate the potential of the switch.

Personally I have experimented with mutual reception as showing a switch with choice in some natal charts with striking and insightful results, so I mention it here as being a point worth further exploration. However, it is still important to consider the condition and dignity of the planets in the sign that they actually occupy.

Other Interpretations of Reception

John Frawley, traditional astrologer and author of "The Real Astrology", uses reception as showing the attitude of the planet being received.

This is the inverse of the classical meaning of reception; it shows the action or attitude of the ruled towards the ruler, the attitude of the house guest towards his or her host.

Frawley uses this very heavily and effectively in his interpretations. So, for example, if Venus is in Cancer, where Jupiter is exalted, Frawley would say that Venus exalts or loves Jupiter. This is a switch from the classical interpretation of reception; here it is the attitude of the ruled planet towards the ruler.

Avelar and Ribeiro, in their classic modern text on traditional astrology, "On the Heavenly Spheres" (p 146) also mention Frawley's interpretation of reception and give an example.

Notice in the following quote that they view reception as working in both directions.

> *(quote from Avelar/Ribeiro)*
> "In practice, we look upon reception as a sign of good will by the dignifying planet to help out the visiting planet...Reception also indicates the predisposition and motivation behind particular actions. A planet that is received in rulership confers great importance onto its dispositor (in the same way that a visitor will honor the host). If the reception occurs through exaltation, it can represent excitement on the part of the planet received."

Though this is not strictly traditional I can see the logic here. Take a planet in Libra. Saturn is exalted in Libra. It makes sense to say that a planet in a house where Saturn is exalted, holds that planet in high regard. There is logic to it.

If you were having a discussion about the merits of The Beatles vs. The Rolling Stones and you lived in a household or domicile where The Stones Rule, you'd probably agree.

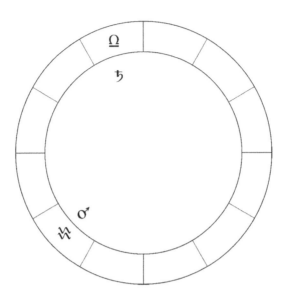

Figure 14: Positive Reception

If there is something to that logic, it could add an interesting twist to reception. However, in practice I find that mixing the two meanings of reception can create confusion.

Take the case of Saturn in Libra with Mars in Aquarius. Saturn rules Aquarius, so he receives Mars, and has obligation to treat Mars well. Saturn is exalted in Libra so he's in good shape. However, Libra, where Saturn resides, is the detriment of Mars. If Frawley and Avelar/Ribeiro are correct, Saturn resides in a house in which Mars is not highly valued, so this negatively impacts Saturn's attitude towards Mars. For me this creates a muddy, contradictory interpretation, as in this case.

On the other hand, Frawley makes very extensive and effective use of this non-traditional sense of reception.

I don't have a definitive answer here. Even though this understanding of reception does not match the strict traditional definition, it is used by some fine traditional astrologers whose opinion I respect. I wanted to mention the two understandings of reception here since I found it very confusing when I was first mastering the concept.

I personally prefer to go with just the classical understanding of reception, and I will use that meaning going forward.

Negative and Mixed Reception

Note that you can also have negative reception, and negative mutual reception For example, Moon in Cancer and Saturn in Capricorn, in opposition by sign. They receive each other into their own detriment, so the two planets would not work together well at all. Both are in their domicile and strong, but working at cross-purposes. Saturn looks down and askance at the Moon as impractical and overly sensitive, and the Moon looks down on strong Saturn as cold and unfeeling. They don't understand each other.

Saturn should be somewhat better received by the Moon since the Moon has dignity by triplicity in earth signs like Capricorn. In that case, the Moon gives Saturn a mixed reception, part dignity, part debility.

Use of Reception

In general, reception is a statement of *how planets influence each other and how they work together*. It describes the quality of the receiving planet towards the planet being received.

Reception should be examined when looking at aspects between planets. The dignities show how they are 'disposed' towards each other. Planets that have some level of mutual reception towards each other are much more likely to cooperate regardless of the nature of the aspect.

Here are two examples here showing the difference that reception makes.

Please see Figure 15 on the next page. In this diagram we have Saturn in Libra square Mars in Capricorn. Saturn receives Mars into his domicile or sign rulership, so Saturn is positively disposed towards Mars. Since aspects are directional and Saturn is the dominant or overcoming planet in this aspect, this means that the action of Saturn towards Mars will be positive for Mars

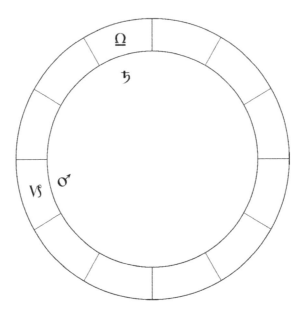

Figure 15: Square with Positive Reception

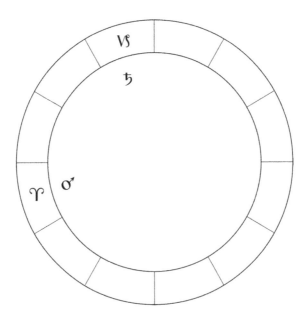

Figure 16: Square with Negative Reception

Please see Figure 16 on the preceding page. In this diagram we have another square, this time of Saturn in Capricorn square Mars in Aries, and again Saturn is the dominant or overcoming planet. However, this time, Saturn receives Mars into his fall, so the action of Saturn on Mars will be more negative or problematic. As a planet in fall, Saturn gives Mars no respect, doesn't listen to Mars, and doesn't pay any attention.

Both of the prior two examples are Saturn square Mars, and reception is the factor that makes all the difference as to how that aspect plays out.

Reception and Planetary Condition

Reception is used to evaluate the condition of a planet in a house. A planet is influenced by the condition of the planets that have rulership and other dignities in the sign where they are placed. If you have a planet that is in difficult condition, you can use the dignities and reception to look for planets that have some authority in that house, to see how it can be positively influenced. We will use that technique in the interpretation section of this book.

So, as in a previous example, Mars in Aquarius is peregrine and has no dignity. That means that Mars is very much at the mercy of Saturn to be able to function well. If Saturn were exalted in Libra, which is trine Aquarius, and receives Mars into a sign he rules, he will likely be well disposed and helpful towards Mars, and Saturn is in good enough shape to have a positive effect. On the other hand, if Saturn were in Leo and opposite Mars, Saturn is in his detriment, hot, cranky and out of sorts, and in no sort of condition to lend any assistance to Mars.

When you have a situation like this, in which the main ruler of a sign is in poor condition, look at the planets that have other dignity in that same sign - exaltation, triplicity, and term - to see if any of those other planets are in better shape, and better able to provide positive support.

Chapter Twenty One:
The Lots or Arabic Parts

Note: *If you are completely new to traditional astrology, the Lots can be considered an advanced topic. It adds quite a bit more complexity to the chart reading. Some people find it easier to set the topic of the Lots aside until after they have mastered the basics of the system.*

Introduction

Most astrologers know the Lots by the name, Arabic Parts. The traditional Hellenistic term was Lot, meaning something like portion or share. Your lot in life is the good or ill fortune you were granted by the Universe, and we still use that term in modern English. Casting Lots was like throwing dice or picking random straws.

They were called Arabic Parts because, other than the Lot of Fortune, they are not referred to in Ptolemy's *Tetrabiblos*, and for a very long time that was the one textbook of Hellenistic astrology that was widely available in the West.

Since the Lots were not in Ptolemy but were widely used in Arabic texts, later astrologers thought that they were an innovation of the Arabs; hence the name Arabic Parts. However, some of the earliest and most influential Greek texts we have, notably those by Dorotheus of Sidon and Paul of Alexandria, use the lots extensively, and they are apparently a key part of the Hellenistic system.

It is now widely accepted that Ptolemy's work is not typical of practicing astrologers of the Hellenistic era. Dorotheus and Paul of Alexandria are considered to be more representative of actual practice. In many ways, what was known as Arabic astrology is closer to actual Hellenistic practice than is Ptolemy.

The Lots were widely used and developed in the Persian and Arabic periods of Astrology. This period built on the tradition of the Hellenistic Lots and also extended it, calculating Lots as needed for diverse subjects. There is logic to how the Lots are constructed, and when you understand the logic you can come up with formulas for new Lots as needed.

Later, in Western Europe, the 13th century medieval astrologer Guido

Bonatti has an extensive catalog of the Lots in his "Book of Astronomy", but does not seem to refer to them widely outside of the one section in which they are listed and described. By the time astrology was translated into Latin and introduced into Europe it appears that the use of the Lots was in decline.

By the time of the Renaissance their use seems to have waned further. From that era, two representative English astrologers were William Lilly and John Gadbury, who were roughly contemporaries. Gadbury, following Bonatti, gives an extensive list of Lots over the space of 4 pages, but, like Bonatti, he does not refer to them outside of that list. On the other hand, following Ptolemy, William Lilly mentions and uses only the Lot of Fortune.

It seems clear that, by that time, the traditional method of using the lots seems to have either fallen into disfavor or been lost. This was partly due to the mistaken conception that, because the Lots were not referred to by Ptolemy, they were not part of the original Hellenistic system.

We are now in a period where contemporary astrologers like Chris Brennan and Dr. Benjamin Dykes, among others, are rediscovering traditional use of the Lots, and they are also being explored in new contexts by other modern astrologers.

Calculating the Lots

In most modern books on astrology that refer to the Lots, they are written in an algebraic formula that looks like this.

A + (B - C) = Lot

For instance, the formula for the Lot of Fortune is usually written as follows.

ASC + (Moon - Sun) = Fortune

However, in the earliest texts, the calculation for the Lot was described something like this: Take the distance from the Sun to the Moon, and cast that same distance off the Ascendant. Or, in the abstract formula, take the distance from point C to point B, and cast that off from point A.

Another way of putting that with Fortune is, The Lot of Fortune is where the Moon would be if the Sun were right on the Ascendant. It is a proportion of relation.

The two ways of calculating the Lots are equivalent, but the traditional method shows more of the logic behind constructing the Lots.

The traditional method of finding the Lots is also more visual. Look at the two planets (at points C and B), and see how far apart they are, and then measure or count the same distance off the Ascendant in the same direction. Since the most important thing about the Lot is which house the Lot falls in, a simple scan is usually sufficient. You only need to calculate the exact degree if the Lot falls near the boundary of a sign.

Reversing the Formula of the Lots

There is one other complication on calculating the lots that again goes back to the influence of Ptolemy on the course of Western astrology.

In both Dorotheus and Paul of Alexandria, sect was a primary factor, and the formula of the Lot was reversed depending on the sect of the chart. That appears to be typical Hellenistic practice, and the reversal of the formula of the Lots is also widely used in Persian and Arabic works.

Ptolemy did not reverse the formula for the Lot of Fortune, and his method became normative in the West. Following Ptolemy, most modern astrologers who use the Part of Fortune do not reverse the calculation for night charts.

In this book, we will be following traditional Hellenistic usage and reversing the formulas for most lots depending on the sect of the chart.

The Lot of Fortune for a diurnal chart is, measure the distance from Sun to Moon, and cast off the Ascendant.

For a nocturnal chart the formula is, measure the distance from Moon to Sun, and cast off the Ascendant. Reverse the direction that you measure from the Sun or Moon.

In both cases, start with the planet of the sect (day or night) and go to the other planet.

There is a reciprocal Lot called the Lot of Spirit, which is the inverse of Fortune. The formula of Spirit for day is, from Moon to Sun, cast off the Ascendant. Reverse the direction for Spirit at night.

It is a statement of common relation, angle, or proportion, and the meaning of the lot seems to include the concept of relation.

Finding the Lots Visually

I want to give some examples here of how you can visually scan for the location of the different lots. Once you understand the principle it is pretty simple, and you will be able to find the lots as you need them without being at the mercy of a computer printout.

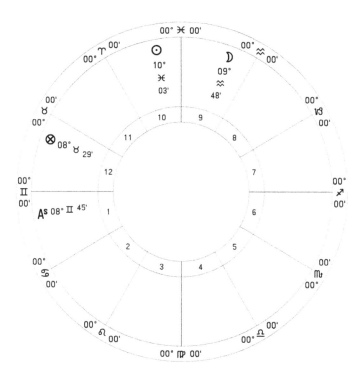

Figure 17: Diurnal Lot of Fortune

The above chart is diurnal, so Lot of Fortune is measured from Sun to Moon. Notice that the Moon is a little bit more than one sign distant, going clockwise. The Lot of Fortune is a little bit more than one sign distant from the Ascendant.

I usually take the shortest distance between the two planets, since it does not matter which way you count that distance. If you measure clockwise from Sun to Moon, then cast off clockwise from the Ascendant, and vice-versa.

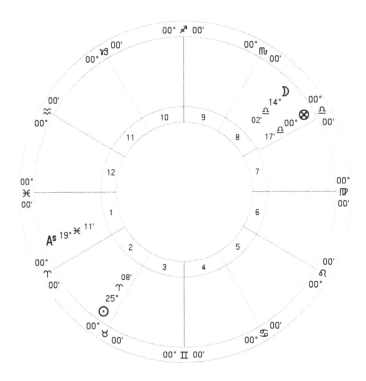

Figure 18: Nocturnal Lot of Fortune

The above chart is nocturnal, so Fortune is measured from the Moon to the Sun. I think going counter-clockwise is easier in this example. Starting at the Moon in Libra, the Sun is about 6 signs or 180 degrees away, plus about another 11 degrees. If you go 180 degrees from the Ascendant you get to 19 Virgo, and adding another 11 degrees puts you in very early Libra.

For the next example please see Figure 18 on the following page.

This chart is nocturnal; Fortune is at 7 Virgo, and Spirit is at 29 Taurus. Notice that they are symmetrically placed on opposite sides of the Ascendant. Fortune is from Moon to Sun, or 4 signs plus 12 degrees clockwise, and Spirit is from Sun to Moon, 4 signs plus 12 degrees counter-clockwise.

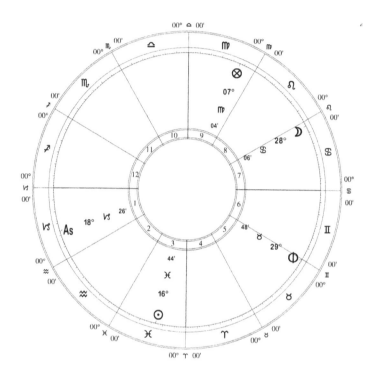

Figure 19: Lots of Fortune and Spirit

Since both Fortune and Spirit use the distance between the Sun and Moon, the position of those two Lots is a function of the moon's phase. A person born under a full moon will have the two Lots approximately opposite the Ascendant; a person born under a new moon will have the two Lots on or very near the Ascendant on either side.

The Geometry of the Lots

In the following sections on the geometry and meaning of the Lots I am drawing on the work of the modern astrologers Lind Weber and David Cochrane.

There is a very important geometric pattern underlying the formula of the Lots, and that pattern seems to underlie both the meaning of the Lots and why they are important and effective in chart interpretation.

If you take the four points that make up the formula of any Lot and connect them, you will always get a geometric structure called an Isosceles Trapezoid, or what you could call a truncated pyramid. The modern harmonic astrologer David Cochrane abbreviates isosceles trapezoid to isotrap, and I will use that term here.

In an isotrap, two of the sides are parallel, and the other two sides are the same length.

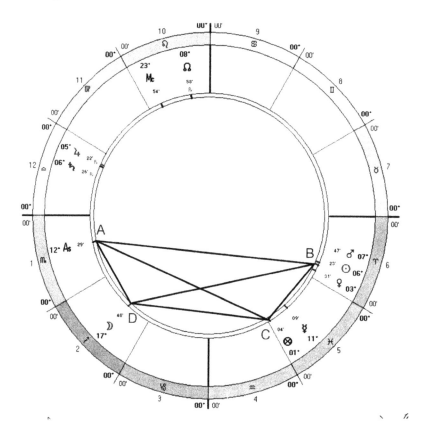

Figure 20: Geometry of the Lots

Here is a diagram of a chart showing the 4 points, Sun, Moon,

Ascendant, and Fortune, and the Isosceles trapezoid formed by the points. This is a nocturnal chart. Line D to B is Moon to Sun; Line A to C is Ascendant to Fortune. The two lines are the same length. That is the definition of the Lot.

Line AD and Line CB are also the same length.

Line AB and line DC are parallel. If you cut Line AB and Line DC in half and connected their midpoints, they would go right through that point where line AC and line DB intersect.

Lots and Harmonic Astrology

There is a very modern form of astrology, called Harmonic astrology that was either invented or discovered in the middle of the 20th century. According to that theory, if two pairs of planets are the same distance apart in degrees, there will be a resonance between them, like two guitar strings of the same length that vibrate together when one is plucked.

The isotrap always creates a pair of such resonances. In our illustration above, it is the two pairs of lines that are the same length. It is like the four points are all activated at once and singing in harmony.

When you have such a structure, *All four points of the isotrap turn on at the same time*.

Importance of Lot of Fortune

This is a primary reason why the Lot of Fortune is so very important.

The point of Fortune is the fourth point of an isotrap waiting to be completed and triggered by transit, direction or synastry.

The location of the Part of Fortune defines the point that completes the interlocking isotrap structure, which inter-relates all the points in the structure.

Any planet that activates the Part of Fortune by transit or direction simultaneously activates the Sun, Moon, and Ascendant and their relationship.

Sun, Moon and Ascendant are the three most important personal points in the chart.

In the book *Arabic Parts Decoded* , Lind Weber maintains that the different Lots, especially the Lot of Fortune, were used for predicting major periods of fortune or misfortune by tracking transits of Jupiter or Saturn to the Lot. From what I have seen this is valid.

Some astrologers maintain that the point of the Lot can be activated by an aspect to the point of the Lot by conjunction, opposition, or square, and some modern astrologers include the eighth harmonic aspects, semisquare and sesquiquadrate.

The Lots and Uranian Astrology

The school of Uranian astrology was started by Alfred Witte in the 1920's. One of the primary techniques that school uses is called, Planetary Pictures, which defines relations between planets that trigger events and have interpretive meaning.

A Planetary Picture is a structure where two sets of midpoints coincide - in other words, an isotrap. The formula for a Uranian Planetary Picture is:

$$A + (B-C) = D, \text{ or, } A/D = C/B$$

That is identical to the formula for calculating Lots.

It is appears that Uranian astrology has rediscovered the geometrical basis and formula that underlies the traditional Lots. This is a case where the most traditional astrology, and the most modern, are converging.

The Planetary Lots

The Lot of Fortune, and its reciprocal point, the Lot of Spirit, are the two most important Lots since they activate the three most important points in the chart. There are also many other Lots that were used.

The Hermetic or Planetary lots appear to have been a primary set, the most basic set of Lots for a chart. Taking the Lot of Fortune as the Lot of the Moon, and the Lot of Spirit as the Lot of the Sun, there are also Lots for each of the other 5 traditional planets. The formula for each of the planetary Lots involves the Ascendant, and either the Lot of Fortune or Spirit.

The names and formulas for diurnal charts of the Hermetic or Planetary Lots are as follows. As with the Lot of Fortune, reverse direction for a nocturnal chart. These versions of the Lots are taken from Paul of Alexandria.

Table 14: Hermetic or Planetary Lots

Planet	Hermetic Name	First Point	Second Point
Mercury	Necessity	Mercury	Fortune
Venus	Eros	Spirit	Venus
Mars	Courage	Mars	Fortune
Jupiter	Victory	Spirit	Jupiter
Saturn	Nemesis	Saturn	Fortune

For a diurnal chart, measure from the first point to the second point and cast off the Ascendant. Reverse the direction for a nocturnal chart.

Note that the benefic planets Venus and Jupiter measure with the Lot of Spirit, and the malefic planets Mars and Saturn measure with the Lot of Fortune. The malefic lots measure from the planet towards Fortune, and the benefic lots measure from Spirit towards the planet. Also note that Mercury is grouped in with the malefics.

In interpreting the meanings of the Planetary lots, Avelar and Ribeiro view each Lot as showing how the nature of the planet tends to play out in the person's life. The Lot of Mars shows how the native experiences the action of the planet Mars in their life, and so on.

If you look at Bonatti's treatise on the Lots, the first section covers the Lots of Fortune and Spirit, which he describes as the Lots of the two Lights, and then the 5 Planetary Lots. Those 7 lots are the primary and most important group. Also, when Bonatti describes the meaning of those lots, he includes a wide spectrum of the planet's meanings, both positive and negative.

In the earliest Greek texts, the old Greek names of the planetary lots were more vivid, and limited in their meaning. By the time of Bonatti, they were just named by planet, and the catalog of meanings for each planetary lot spans the gamut of the meaning for that planet.

I find that the broader meaning of the planetary lots works out better in practice than the more limited original Greek meaning.

Lots as Relation

The formula for calculating a lot shows relation - for instance, the Lot of Fortune shows a relationship of the Ascendant, which is the native that reflects the relationship from the Sun to the Moon.

Using the metaphor of relation, the Lot shows how the person *relates to* that planet or subject in their life. There seems to be a strong psychological or attitude component. The Lot shows how the native experiences or relates to the subject area described by the Lot, especially how the native experiences the Lot's subject internally.

Robert Zoller, who wrote a definitive modern work on the Lots, interprets the Lots of Fortune and Spirit as having a strong spiritual and psychological component. Zoller views them as expressing the inner world of the native, while the usual meaning of planets in traditional astrology shows the outer expression.

Other Lots

There are many, many, other Lots on all sorts of specific topics, from Marriage to Death to Fornication to Lentils. (The Arabs used lots on specific products like lentils to predict commodity prices.)

As with the seven Hermetic Lots, the Lots on specific subjects have a strong sense of personal experience, how the person relates to the Lot's topic. For instance, the lot of the Father shows how I view or experience my father in my life, what my relationship to my father is like.

Here is a short starting list of some Lots that are generally useful in natal interpretation. The formulas are given for diurnal charts; reverse direction for a nocturnal chart.

Table 15: Other Commonly Used Lots

Lot Name	First Point	Second Point
Father	Sun	Saturn
Mother	Venus	Moon
Children	Jupiter	Saturn
Friends	Moon	Venus
Work	Mercury	Mars
Marriage *	Saturn	Venus

For a diurnal chart, measure from the first point to the second point and cast off the Ascendant. Reverse the direction for a nocturnal chart.

* Note that the Lot of Marriage is a bit more complex in that it is reversed for day or night as usual, but it is also reversed for Women.

So, for the Lot of Marriage for Men shown in the table above, cast from Saturn to Venus off Ascendant. Reverse at night.

For the Lot of Marriage for Women, cast from Venus to Saturn off the Ascendant. Reverse at night.

For a more extensive list of traditional lots, you can consult either Ben Dykes, *Introductions to Traditional Astrology*, or Al-Biruni, *The Book of Instruction in the Elements of the Art of Astrology*. Some of the Lots have more than one formula. There are also newer lots using the 3 modern outer planets, and most modern astrology programs provide an extensive list.

Interpreting a Lot

To interpret a lot's meaning in traditional astrology, consider the following factors.

- The location of the Lot by house and sign, with house being much more significant than sign.

- The ruler of the lot by sign, location, condition. Note that some traditional sources view the ruler's location, condition and aspects as more important than the location and aspects of the lot itself.

- Other planets in the house of the Lot. If there is a planet in the same house, it can be interpreted in the same way as the ruling planet.

- Other planets in the Stakes or in aspect to the lot.

- Pay special attention to the planet in closest aspect to the ruler of the lot, and the planet most closely aspecting the lot itself.

- Whether the house of the lot is angular, succedent or cadent will affect how the lot manifests.

Lots can have accidental dignity by house location or planets aspecting it. An angular lot will be more visible in effect, a lot aspected by Jupiter will be more fruitful for good fortune.

Lots do not have essential dignity since by definition they are in the house of their ruler, but the dignities effective at the lot's location can show other planet's influence on the lot's expression.

More on the Lot of Fortune

I want to examine the Lot of Fortune further since it can be so important in chart interpretation.

Going back to a traditional source, Bonatti calls Fortune, the Part of the Moon. In good condition it it often signifies material good fortune. Things happen to you here, for good or ill.

In profections or other time lord systems, which are predictive methods of moving the chart forward in time, having the active house for the period be in the stakes to the lot will make the year eventful - a lot will happen to you in that year.

I have seen Fortune interpreted as signifying where your happiness is, or where you desire to be fortunate.

Taking the Lots in general as having psychological or relational component, then Fortune can be interpreted in a wider sense as being 'where your fortune is', or what part of your life you seek to be fortunate.

It seems to be related to happiness, to what makes you happy, what you most value.

The Lot refers to what is fortunate in a wider sense - I was fortunate to marry who I did, or, fortunate to end up working as a musician, or whatever. Fortune seems to have something to do with fulfilling the heart's desire. There is definitely a material dimension to Fortune, but it does not exhaust the meaning of the lot.

When you delineate the lot, the location and condition of the Lot's ruler can tell you a lot about how that part of your life will go, how likely you are to fulfill that fortune you want.

And following on that - when Fortune is activated, through profection or other direction, by transit or by synastry with another person, it is likely that the activity will be related to whatever area that person's fortune lies. Not just busy, but busy related to Fortune's subject.

In a natal chart in which any planet is conjunct Fortune or Spirit, that planet plays a very strong part in that person's overall character. The isotrap structure of the lot is already built internally, and does not need to wait to be triggered by a transit or synastry. For a person who has a planet conjunct Fortune in the natal, there is a sense they *make their own Fortune* for good or ill.

The reciprocal Lot of Spirit seems to signify spiritual vocation, or work you are called to do. Bonatti calls it the Pars Futurorum - part of things to come - or, the part of the Sun.

The Lot of Spirit is also relational, and like Fortune, important things happen when something touches that point.

The Lots in the Interpretation Examples

Much of the meaning of the various Lots is internal rather than situational, and has to do with how the person relates to the Lot's topic. The Lots do not reflect the outer persona, but the inner experience. For that reason, when looking at a celebrity chart, it is often hard or impossible to determine the Lot's significance since it is not visible.

I find that they very often add an extra dimension of meaning. They are worth taking the time to feel out and explore.

Part Two:

Evaluation, Interpretation

and Examples

Section Five: Evaluation and Interpretation

Chapter Twenty Two:
Evaluation Rules

Introduction

Before you can interpret how a planet will act, you need to get an idea of the condition the planet is in. This section of the book considers how that evaluation is done in traditional astrology.

Evaluating Essential and Accidental Dignities

Essential dignity refers to the 5 categories of dignity or rulership, ruler, exalted, triplicity, term and face, that a planet has from occupying a specific degree in a sign. Essential dignity is said to determine the quality of the planet's action.

All of the other kinds of dignities are situational, and refer to such things as house position, angularity, speed and direction, and different kinds of aspects to other planets. All these other conditions are called accidental dignities, and are said to affect ability of the planet to act, its visibility and power.

So, essential dignities are quality, accidental are visibility and power, ability and opportunity to act.

However, the more I think about it, if you examine the various accidental dignities, I don't think that division holds up. A lot of the accidental dignities affect the quality of action also.

Take even the most straightforward measurement of power, which is angularity. Planets near an angle are said to be strong, active and external, and planets far from an angle are called cadent and weak. However, cadent planets are not just weak, they act in a different way, more internally and more related to reflection than to action. That is as much a difference in quality as in power.

For another example, take a retrograde planet. Yes, that does affect the strength of a planet's action, but it also affects the nature and quality of that action - it may be more internal, and may impede, or delay, and sometimes quite strongly.

And finally, take aspects. Any planet making a hard aspect to Saturn won't just be weakened, but be changed in type and quality of action.

So, when you refer to traditional texts, you will see the terms essential dignity (the 5 kinds of rulership) and accidental dignity (all the other situational characteristics). My own opinion is that you need to evaluate the quality and effect of each condition separately, rather than just combining them all under ability to act.

The following list of negative and positive conditions - the infortunes and fortunes of the planets - is from a book from the late 1500's titled, *The Judgment of Nativities*, by Augur Ferrier. It is very similar to comparable lists in Bonatti, Lilly and other writers. I have omitted some of the less important conditions.

At the end of the chapter, after the lists of fortunes and infortunes, there is a note on the special condition called heliacal rising or setting.

Note: *I am keeping some of the archaic language and spelling from the original.*

Here Followeth The Infortunes of the Planets

When burned under the beams of the Sun (combust and under the rays)

This was considered one of the worst debilities for a planet. The Sun is the largest and brightest of the planets, so any planet moving close to it is completely hidden under its bright ray - combust means burnt. It's like the Sun sucks all the life out of the planet and leaves it little power to act independently. The planet is fried.

The full condition of being Combust is within 8 degrees of the Sun. A planet between 8 and 15 degrees from the Sun is called, Under the Sun's Beams (USB) - meaning not quite visible but not quite completely fried either. The planet is debilitated and weakened, but not as completely as if it were combust.

When you have this condition, it is worth noting to see if the planet is approaching or separating from the Sun. Obviously, approaching means the condition is getting worse.

Because a planet close to the Sun is hidden, being combust or under the rays also connotes being hidden, out of awareness, sometimes out of control. If secrecy is desired this can be a positive condition.

A planet that is either combust or under the rays is inhibited in its ability to act independently.

I think the keyword here is, *independently*. From what I've seen in charts a planet conjunct the Sun isn't necessarily weak, but it cannot act by itself. Also, depending on the planet, it can have an effect on how the Sun acts in the chart.

A lot depends on the planet's dignities here. A planet having good essential dignity is said not to be weakened by being under the Sun.

This also depends on the nature of the planet. I have seen Mars, which is hot and dry, be quite strong and even inflamed when conjunct the Sun, though still not able to act independently of the Sun, and out of awareness and control.

Cool, moist Venus seems to be quite weakened conjunct the Sun if not in good essential dignity.

Saturn conjunct the Sun is ugly, but more so for the Sun than for Saturn. The hot, dry Sun needs to shine, and Saturn conjunct is a cold, dark, rigid dry wall of stone blocking the shining. Staying with that same metaphor, it often means that a person was blocked from shining in some way, possibly as a child, hence a block on self-expression. Or, the furnace of the Sun could crack the wall, so there is the sense of controlled energy that could burst out. The dignity of Saturn makes a lot of difference in how this plays out, but the two planets are such direct opposites that it is at best a difficult merger.

Also, remember that the Sun's and Saturn's dignities and debilities are opposite each other, so when they are conjunct they cannot both be dignified, and often one or the other of them is debilitated.

Being combust or under the beams affects a planet's ability to act visibly and effectively in external circumstances. Since traditional astrology focuses on external events and actions - exclusively so in the older texts - this is a serious debility.

Older traditional astrology does not address the whole issue of how this affects the inner life or character of the native. In another area, modern astrology has added the connotation of retrograde as an energy that could be reversed, in the sense of turned inward. I wonder if something similar might apply to planets burned by the Sun or under the rays, especially if other circumstances supported it - i.e., if it were in a cadent house or a mutable sign. Perhaps a combust planet could be very intense internally, but not easily in awareness. Any planet conjunct the Sun is too close to the source of light to be seen.

Note that there is a special condition called, *Cazimi,* which means, at the heart of the Sun. If the conjunction is very tight - within 1 degree of conjunct in older texts, within 17 minutes in later ones - then instead of being a debility, it is the strongest dignity that can happen to the planet. The planet is located right at the Heart of the King, and so is super fortunate.

The singer and performer Harry Belafonte has Jupiter in Pisces in his rulership, Cazimi the Sun, in the 10th house of maximum visibility. Charisma!

The crucial point in any form of conjunction to the Sun is that the planet is taken up into the energy of the Sun so that it does not have a separate identity or action.

Retrograde and First Station - When a planet is retrograde it appears to be going in the opposite direction of the usual motion of the planets. Think of the words you'd associate with opposite motion and you'll get a good feel for what retrograde signifies - opposite, contrary, ornery, going against the grain, opposed, backing up, retreating.

The worst kind of retrograde condition is right when the planet is slowing down and starting to turn around and back up. This is called the first station, and it is a serious debility. Planets in station are intensified because they are basically just pausing and standing still. If being retrograde is an illness, then first station is when you take to your sickbed.

Retrograde is considered a serious debility in traditional astrology, especially since it places a high value on going with the expected order, and a retrograde planet is moving against the grain, out of order.

A retrograde planet impedes, delays, holds back, weakens, inhibits and reverses. Besides a restriction or delay on expression, a retrograde planet may act counter to expectations - so ornery, contrary, rebellious, going against the grain.

Retrograde definitely affects how quickly, directly and predictably a planet acts.

Retrograde can also mean that the external action of the planet is inhibited, and its energy is turned inward. It is more hesitating, doubting, and perhaps introspective.

In their detriment or fall - that was covered in the chapter on essential dignities.

In declining houses - declining is another word for cadent houses - the word cadent literally means falling away. This makes it hard for the planet to be visible or to act directly. We have noted, in the chapter on the houses, that sometimes the action of a cadent planet is either more hidden or more internal.

The one exception to this rule is the ninth house. While it is cadent, this house is viewed as more fortunate than the other cadent houses. There seem to be two factors at play here. The first is that this house is very elevated, right at the top of the chart, and planets gain strength by being elevated. The second is that this house makes a strong trine to the Ascendant by whole sign aspect, so planets here are strongly situated relative to the Ascendant.

Conjunct the South Node - the South Node is considered to be of the nature of Saturn in traditional astrology. It is an energy sink, and sucks the life out of any planet near it.

Aspected by a retrograde planet The ill effects of a retrograde planet also affects those planets that it aspects. In traditional astrology we would look at those planets aspecting a point by whole signs from the stakes, meaning in square or opposition by sign.

Peregrine **without reception** *by the sign ruler* - Since the ruler, by definition, receives the peregrine planet in domicile, I take this to mean that there has to be an aspect with the ruler. At the very least the ruler cannot be averse. An in orb degree aspect is stronger than a whole sign aspect, but either kind of aspect alleviates this condition. This is part of the larger rule that a peregrine planet's condition very much depends on the location, condition and aspect of the planet's Lord.

When not aspecting any other planet - This is called being Feral, and means that the planet does not make any major aspect with the planet - conjunction, sextile, square, trine or opposition. This can be either by degree aspect, meaning no other planet is within orb, or by whole sign, a much rarer and much worse condition. A planet which is feral is considered to be like a wild animal, outside of the civilizing and integrating influence of aspects to other planets. It can act very strongly but is not integrated, and is difficult to control.

When opposite to the Lord of the sign they are in - By definition this would put their ruler in detriment and therefore in bad condition.

Besieged between two evill Planets - this is a special condition called being besieged, where a planet is separating from a degree aspect from one of the malefics, and applying to a degree aspect with the other. It's like being between a rock and a hard place. Things go from bad to worse.

In the 12th sign from a house they rule - e.g., Moon rules Cancer and would be disadvantaged in Gemini. Mercury rules Gemini and Virgo, and thus would be disadvantaged in Taurus and Leo. I have seen this condition widely used in traditional texts with the Moon in Gemini, and not as widely noted with other planets.

Out of sect - already covered.

Masculine in a feminine sign, and vice-versa. I do not consider this a very important condition since each planet other than the Sun or Moon each rules one masculine and one feminine sign.

Infortunes particular to the Moone

When She Decreaseth - The moon waning. In the cycle of the Moon's phases, a waxing or increasing Moon is getting stronger, larger, brighter, and more manifest. A waning moon is decreasing, getting darker, smaller, gradually extinguishing.

The Moon in the 8th house with no dignity. Any planet in the eighth house is considered to be debilitated, since it is averse the Ascendant and has difficulty being seen or acting. This was considered to be especially debilitating for the Moon in the eighth house. Notice, however, that if the Moon has dignity in the sign she is in, that alleviates the worst effect of being in the eighth house.

The Fortunes of the Planets

In angular or succedent houses - these are houses where planets are strong, visible and able to act.

Note one important exception to this rule, which is the eighth house. Even though that house is succedent, it does not aspect the ascendant and is considered malefic.

In good aspect to Jupiter or Venus, with reception - aspects from *any* planet, benefic or malefic, depend primarily on condition and reception to evaluate their effect.

Cazimi, at the heart of the Sun - this was discussed earlier in the section on combustion. A planet in very tight conjunction with the Sun was considered to be very fortunately favored, at the heart of the king.

In good aspect to Sun, Moon or Mercury when they are dignified. When a planet was in conjunction, sextile or trine to one of these three planets, they were considered to act as benefics and have a favorable effect.

Conjunct the North Node - The North Node is of the nature of the benefic Jupiter, and will tend to increase or magnify the power of any planet near it.

Note that this is not always a good thing. If you have a malefic planet in bad condition near the North Node, its ability to cause mischief is increased.

Direct, or in second station - Just as a planet in first station is particularly debilitated, a planet in second station is getting reading to Turn Its Life Around and Get Moving.

In their rulership or exaltation - A planet having a major dignity is considered strengthened.

In two of the minor dignities - Having two of the minor dignities is considered as strong as having one of the major dignities.

Using the system of five dignities, a planet in either its domicile or rulership is dignified and benefitted. The other, minor dignities are considered important if a planet is in two or more of them. For instance, a planet which was in its own triplicity and terms would be considered dignified in the same way as a planet in either domicile or exaltation. A single minor dignity is not considered as important, but it does keep a planet from being peregrine.

In houses where they 'naturally take pleasure' . This could be interpreted in two different senses.

- In the house in which they have their joy. We discussed that in the section on the Joy of the Planets in the chapter on houses.

- Or, in Morin's phrase, this is a planet in a house in which they have an analogy or affinity to the domain of the house. For instance, the 2nd house has to do with money and possessions, and Jupiter has an analogy to that meaning, so Jupiter would naturally take pleasure in the second house in that sense.

Peregrine if received - a planet with no essential dignity relies completely on its ruler. To be received, the planet must be in whole sign aspect with its ruler. You can then look at the location and condition of the ruler to further determine how helpful it will be.

At the highest part of their Circles, meaning elevated or near the top of the chart, in either the ninth or tenth house.

Emerging from under the beams of the Sun , meaning the planet is exiting being under the Sun's Beams and becoming visible. See the note on heliacal rising below.

In their proper sect - this was discussed in the chapter on sect.

In sign of matching gender - The Sun, Mars, Jupiter and Saturn are considered masculine, and are benefitted by being in the masculine fire or air signs. The Moon and Venus are considered feminine, and are benefitted by being in the feminine earth or water signs. Mercury rising before the Sun is considered Masculine, and rising after the Sun is considered feminine.

Benefics in the stakes of the planet, aspecting it by whole sign by opposition or square. Even though the opposition and square are considered difficult aspects, having an aspect from Venus or Jupiter is fortunate - but again, this depends on the condition of the planet and whether there is reception.

Particular Fortune of the Moone

When she increaseth, or is waxing. A waxing moon is getting stronger, brighter, more manifest and powerful.

Heliacal Rising and Setting

There is another significant planetary condition to note, that was used in Hellenistic astrology. We mentioned that a planet less than 15 degrees from the Sun was Under the Sun's Beams and so not visible. If a planet emerges from that condition within two weeks of a person's birth, it is said to be making a *Heliacal Rising*, meaning it is coming out from under the Sun and becoming visible. Think of a planet making a heliacal rising as calling attention to itself, waving its planetary hands and saying, Hey, Notice Me!

The opposite condition, *Heliacal Setting*, is when a planet is entering into the Sun's rays within two weeks of birth. The planet is dropping out of notice, going hidden, being eclipsed by the Sun

Table 16: Dignity and Debility Summary List

This is a shorthand list of positive and negative points to scan for when evaluating a planet's condition.

Positive Conditions	Negative Conditions
Cazimi (conjunct Sun)	Combust, Under the Rays
Direct, second Station	Retrograde, first station
In rulership or exaltation, or 2 minor dignities	In detriment or fall
In angular or succedent Houses	In cadent Houses
Strong by angularity	Cadent by angularity
Conjunct North Node	Conjunct South Node
Peregrine, but received by ruler in good condition	Peregrine without reception by ruler
In good aspect to other planets	Feral, not aspecting any other planet
	Opposite the ruler of its sign; the ruler would be in detriment
Surrounded by benefics, or leaving aspect of malefic and approaching aspect of benefic	Besieged by 2 malefics, or leaving aspect of benefic and approaching aspect of malefic
Heliacal rising	Heliacal setting
In sign of matching gender	In sign of opposite gender
Moon waxing	Moon waning
	Moon in 8th house with no dignity
In good aspect to Jupiter or Venus with reception; or, good aspect to dignified Sun, Moon or Mercury with reception	In difficult aspect to Mars or Saturn without reception
In the house of their joy; or a house having analogy by meaning	In a house without analogy by meaning
In sect	Out of sect
In the stakes with benefics	In the stakes with malefics
aspecting its ruler	averse to its ruler

Chapter Twenty Three:
Interpretation Principles from Morin

In this chapter we begin to make the transition from looking at evaluation, to looking at meaning or interpretation.

Once you have looked at the planets and gotten an idea of their condition, you then need to consider how to interpret the meaning of the planets, where and how they will act. We need an interpretive framework to use for that purpose.

Astrologia Gallica Book 21 - Required Reading

Fortunately there is an outstanding traditional text that does just that. It is Book 21 of Astrologia Gallica, which was a massive, multi volume treatise written by the Renaissance era French astrologer Jean-Baptiste Morin, known in Latin as Morinus.

If there is a single book on traditional astrology that you need to study, this is it. It is an absolutely astounding, clear and practical synthesis of reasoned principles of interpretation. I've read it through something like ten times now and I keep learning new things.

This chapter is a very, very brief introduction to the core principles of the Morinus system of chart interpretation. It is very brief and compressed, and each point could make a good topic of a meditation.

I think it will give you enough to get started, but I cannot emphasize enough the necessity to go to the original source.

Principles from Morin

Here is my attempt to take Morin's interpretive system and introduce it as a usable, simple set of basic principles.

1) planets act primarily in the houses they are in.

2) planets have effect in the house(s) they rule.

3) planets are also affected by planets in the houses they rule, so the effect goes both ways.

4) Any planet is affected by

     a) other planets in the same house.

     b) its house ruler and/or house almuten, the planet with the most dignity affecting that house.

     c) other planets aspecting it, especially those from the Stakes.

Everything else is derived from those core principles, depending on the condition, location, and interaction of the planets involved.

Remember that, when you evaluate a planet's condition, you need to take into account both essential dignity (quality), and accidental dignity (power and ability to act).

Principle of Analogy

Morin introduces the principle of analogy of a planet to the house it is acting in. Analogy means something like sympathy, or likeness of purpose and style.

Let Jupiter be in the second house. Even though Jupiter has no specific association with the second house, it shares a quality of abundance with the second house of wealth. So, you would say that Jupiter has analogy with the second house, so its action will be increased in benefit.

If you had Saturn in the second house, Saturn's effect is to limit and impede, and it can be associated with lean times or even poverty. Saturn does not have analogy with the second house, so either its good action is decreased or it is more likely to be malefic.

This does not mean that Saturn cannot be turned to positive effect here, but it takes work to reap the serious Saturn virtues.

Jupiter in second house is generally a lot more Fun than Saturn.

Analogy can be used between

a) a planet and the house it is in.

b) a planet and the house it rules.

c) houses otherwise connected by rulership or aspects. An aspect from the 11th house to the 2nd would be strengthened in good effect since the two houses have analogy as houses of good fortune. Their purposes work together.

Evaluation of Condition

Once you have weighed up all of the dignities and debilities of a planet's position, the following common-sense rules apply.

benefics in good shape produce serious and ongoing good fortune.

benefics in so-so shape produce some good fortune, but not as consistently or strongly, intermittently, and sometimes with some ill effects.

When benefics are in poor shape, the good fortune falls apart, can be negative or create promises that do not fulfill. This is a place in which a benefic can function as what is called an accidental malefic.

A malefic in good shape will produce eventual good fortune, but with hard work and setbacks. Regardless of how good its condition, Saturn is still Saturn, and Mars is still Mars. This would be a case of a malefic planet functioning as an accidental benefic.

A malefic in so-so shape is definitely Not Fun, a source of bad fortune, probably intermittently.

With a malefic in bad shape you will likely see serious and continuous bad fortune, a malefic that is strong in malice. This does not necessarily mean evil, but the effect of a planet that is strongly malefic will be very difficult to turn to positive account even with a great deal of effort and good will, and may very well just be malefic and out of a person's control. I know that is hard for some modern people to accept, astrologer or not, but it is realistic. Sometimes a malefic is just malefic. We do not control all good and ill fortune in our lives. Nor do we deserve all the ill fortune that happens to us; sometimes bad things happen to good people.

I think it is very important to drop all notion of blame when dwelling with misfortune from the malefics. If something bad happens to you, this does not mean that it is your fault or that you necessarily could have done otherwise. Associating misfortune and blame can lead to destructive guilt and shame.

In almost all cases, the condition of a planet is somewhere in between the two extremes, with good points and bad points, a mixture of dignity and debility.

That is where the fun comes in, where you weigh up those good and bad points to see how the qualities can all work together. If you get a feel for how each of the dignities and debilities work separately, then you can create a detailed and nuanced picture of how they combine.

Pairs of Houses

Morin often talks about the houses in opposite pairs, and how planets in one house affect the affairs of the opposite house. And, anything that affects one house is colored in meaning by its opposite.

This is also a general principle of how the house meanings are defined. If you take them in pairs, their relative meanings have affinity with each other.

I think this is related to the stakes, the opposition/ square /cross formation, as a general interpretive principle. Here, Morin is talking about the *subject* of action rather than planetary influence or power.

Order of Planets

Morin talks about the order of benefics and malefics, but the principle applies to the order of planets in general.

If Jupiter is in an earlier degree of a house and Saturn is in a later degree, the effect will be to have good fortune followed by misfortune. Or, if a planet first aspects a malefic and then aspects a benefic, there will be misfortune followed by good fortune.

This makes sense if you consider that directions or transiting planets will fire off the aspects to planets in degree order.

Particularly with multiple planets in a single house, the order of the planets says something about the order of how they act, with the final planet being an outcome or final expression. You can read the sequence of planets in order like a story.

Houses Connected

Houses can be connected by subject depending on planetary rulership.

There is a connection between the house a planet is in, and the house(s) that it rules, and each of those affects the others.

Take Mars in Gemini in the 5th house, which gives Aquarius rising. In this case, the affairs of the 5th house can be tied up with the affairs of the 3rd house (Aries) and 10th (Scorpio), since those are the houses that Mars rules. The career (10th) could be related to children, creativity or leisure activities (5th).

Whenever planets interact – in conjunction, in rulership, in any kind of aspect - take into account their reception based on their dignities. I think the dignity and reception shapes the aspect quality more than the type of aspect.

Planetary Power and Effect

 A planet's action is most powerful in the house where it is located. Morin uses the word powerful, and the astrologer Ben Dykes uses the word immediate instead of powerful. I think the two words catch slightly different dimensions of the meaning.

A planet is affected by the house it is in, but it is also affected by the condition of its ruler. When you have a planet/ruler relationship like this, a planet can manifest as the start of matter, while the ruler determines the quality of final outcome. A planet in poor shape, ruled by a planet in good shape, could mean that affairs of this house start out poorly but turn out well. The reverse condition also applies.

Chapter Twenty Four:
Aphorisms

We have all the pieces in place, we have a set of interpretive principles. Before we go on to our interpretation outline, there are some interesting observations that we have not covered, and this chapter is devoted to them.

Many of the traditional astrology texts have chapters which are just called, aphorisms, and are miscellaneous short paragraphs of various interpretive gems of wisdom. Often they are some of the best material in the text. For instance, Guido Bonatti's short chapter of 146 Considerations is by far the most well known section of his entire massive book, and one of the richest in meaning.

Following in the footsteps of my revered ancestors, this chapter consists of thoughts and observations that should be of use in traditional chart interpretation.

If multiple planets aspect a single other planet or point, look at the order in time that those aspects perfect to describe a sequence or process.

Similarly, when there is more than one planet in a house, consider the degree order of the planets as a sequence or process - that is the order that planets will be triggered by direction, progression or transit. The earliest planet by degree in the house will initiate the process, and the latest planet concludes it.

--

A planet in a late degree of a sign is usually considered a debility. There seem to be two reasons for this.

First, it is in terms or bounds of the malefics - the final degrees of every sign have either Mars or Saturn as bound lord.

Second, the planet's position in late degrees is considered unstable; it is not quite fully in its current sign, but not yet transitioned to the next sign.

--

In building your interpretations, stay simple, stay concrete - start with the most basic meanings and build from there. Always take into account the building blocks (sect, hot/cold/dry/wet, cardinal/fixed/mutable, angular/succedent/ cadent, the basic planetary and house meanings), and let the interpretation emerge from that.

--

The ruler of the house determines the source or cause of the results of that house. For example, if the ruler of the 2nd house is in the 10th, then 2nd house finances are the result of 10th house matters.

So, a planet acts in the house it is in, and its final effect or outcome is in the house(s) it rules.

A planet is also affected by any planets in the houses it rules. The effect is not one way; it is reciprocal.

To give an example of the previous 3 points, take Saturn in Libra in the 10th house, ruling Capricorn in the first and Aquarius in the second, with Venus in Aquarius in the 2nd. Saturn in the 10th house (malefic) acts immediately in 10th (hindrances to career), and this affects the houses it rules - 1st(hurts self esteem) and 2nd(limits income). Saturn is also affected by Venus in ruled 2nd house - the career (10th) could take on a Venusian or artistic quality, or be softened, or have a human relations side (Venus ruling Libra in 10th).

--

One of the most valuable lessons I have learned from traditional astrology, and its sometimes stoic attitude towards acceptance of the difficult parts of human life, is this.

There is a difference between fatalism and mature adult acceptance of limitation.

Denial of the possibility of anything negative happening is actually a kind of spiritual immaturity. Whether we like it or not, one of the rules of this crazy planet we live on seems to be that some of the greatest gifts in life come out of some of the greatest suffering. Trying to deny the suffering shuts us off from some of its greatest gifts.

Do not try to shield your client from the problems you see in their chart That is both disrespectful and condescending - you are implying that they are so weak and sensitive that they cannot bear to have things not go their way. Frame your feedback respectfully and gently, but give your client accurate feedback.

You rob yourself when you try to deny your own source of suffering. You rob others when you shield them.

--

Planets in a house are BOTH the external events and people signified by that house, AND how the person relates to that part of their lives. I think you get the most accurate and grounded interpretation if you start with the externals, but both aspects of the planet's meaning are necessary.

I find that Mercury is almost always a critical planet for understanding the native's character, more so than any other planet. Mercury rules their consciousness, how they use their minds.

Astrology is not mind reading. It needs a context of the native's life circumstances to flesh out the interpretation. The initial scan of the chart, before feedback, provides a kind of frame that can be filled when you know some of the facts of the person's life. For me, the real reading does not start until I get a feel for the chart in context.

You do not need to be intuitive or psychic to be able to accurately interpret astrology charts, and unlike some modern approaches, traditional astrology is not framed as a training ground for psychic intuition. Follow the rules, learn the procedures, and stay within that framework. I find that when I try to take an intuitive leap out of the framework, I leap off into nowhere and go wildly wrong.

Without feedback on the actual circumstances of a person's life, there is a limit to how specific an interpretation you can offer. Mars in the 10th house means that this person's 10th house experiences (career, their supervisors, people in control over them, and their reputation) will have a martial quality. Without feedback you can describe those martial qualities in general terms, but not predict the exact form that martial quality will manifest.

Think of going through the essential dignities as showing the person's assigned place in the order of the universe.

Just as the planets and the stars have their place in that order, so do we have our place.

The question to ask the chart is not, what can I make of my life thanks to or despite my chart, but rather, what does my chart tell me about my assigned role, and how can I fulfill that role.

It is a Stoic kind of acceptance of one's destiny from the Gods in a gracious and mature way.

To paraphrase Viktor Frankl, it is not we that ask what the meaning of life is, but the events of Life that ask that question of us. We are born into an existing order we do not control, and our life's challenge is to respond with meaning to our place in that order.

--

The Wounded Planet. Often, if a single planet is particularly debilitated, it can become a focus of the native's life. Learning to make that problem planet work, coping with it, can become one of the native's main sources of strength.

People who do healing have most power to heal where they have been wounded themselves. I think something like that often happens with problem planets.

--

When interpreting a chart for a person, it is worth starting by asking, Why are you here? What concern is on your mind? What drives you to have your chart interpreted just now? This defining question can become a framework for interpreting the chart. Most of traditional astrology is framed along the lines of answering specific questions rather than looking for vague generalities. So, ask the question.

--

Drawing up a chart for the time of consultation can often give insight into the issues on the client's mind when seeking a reading. This is a technique that has strong roots in both traditional and modern astrology. I have found it to be very helpful.

If you do draw up a consultation chart, look especially for any planets in the first house, the ruler of the first, and the position and condition of the moon, for information on what the focus of the reading will be.

--

Check for planets in close proximity to the Nodes. A planet near the North Node is magnified, and can be increased in importance. A planet near the South Node is decreased or debilitated, and this can decrease its power and effectiveness.

--

Check for planets in close proximity to the part of Fortune or of Spirit. Since those points have a close connection to Sun, Moon and Ascendant they are critical to the person. Someone having a planet on one of those lots makes their own fortune, it is built in to their character.

--

Check the degrees that planets occupy. If you have several planets all at the same degree number give or take 1 or 2, then any transit or direction that sets off one will set off the others by aspect. Inspect the relationship of those planets because the native likely has their issues all activated at the same time.

Or if you have planets all within a small range of degree numbers, then those planets will be triggered in sequence.

When looking at essential dignities and debilities, a strongly debilitated planet can be as potent in its own difficult way, as a strongly dignified planet in an opposite way. Saturn in his fall in Aries, and Mars in his fall in Cancer, can be particularly potent for misfortune depending on house placement and aspects.

Think of the principle of balance. If you minimize or gloss over the difficult and negative parts of a chart, it ends up damping down the positive parts. You get a vague and bland mix somewhere in the middle.

Human life varies from near divine on one end to hellish horror on the other. Our astrology needs to be big enough to encompass both with open eyes.

--

The fifth house is joy of Venus, which is why artistic, Venusian endeavor belongs in this house.

So a writer from the fifth house would be a teller of tales for amusement or beauty, hence poet, storyteller. Similarly, a planet in the fifth house could signify music as pastime, pleasure or enjoyment.

Writing per se as medium of communication or ideas is related to the 3rd/9th house axis, which is related to teaching and philosophy.

The fifth house as creativity is a modern concept, and it seems to be connected to the Venusian side of this house.

--

The second house as 'values' rather than possessions is too vague - I think values in the sense of strongly held moral codes or convictions align better with the 3rd/9th axis.

However, also look for the Lot of Fortune for what a person holds close to their heart, one of their prime values.

--

Saturn in the twelfth house is in his joy, and has analogy with the meaning of the house. So, even though it is a cadent house, Saturn can be quite strong in effect from the twelfth, but it is not an action that the native will be aware of or be able to consciously control or influence. By definition the house is averse to the ascendant, so not visible.

--

Be specific - you will have some interpretations turn out wrong. Share them anyway; let the chart speak for itself. When an interpretation doesn't fall out right, try to figure out why. This is often part of the initial, 'feeling things out' phase of doing a reading.

Part of learning to interpret charts well, is learning to trust that what the chart is actually saying to you is trustworthy.

I have repeatedly seen a planet being out of sect as meaning related to a group that is out of power, not respected, out of fashion.

••

I think the third and fourth houses are both related to family and early environment.

--

Another interpretation of a planet in fall - we said this meant the planet felt it was not being respected, not heard or seen, not taken seriously. Sometimes this can mean that a person with a planet in fall will act with that planet as if other people could not see what they were doing, whether they could or not. So, they could be going merrily along doing things they thought were secret, that everyone around them was aware of but didn't say anything.

For example, a person with Venus in fall could be married and having an affair, thinking that it was completely secret, while their spouse and many of their friends knew about it.

Chapter Twenty Five:
Introduction to Interpretation Outline

If interpreting a chart is like building a house, in Part One of this book I gave you the parts and the tools - hammer, nails, boards, glass and so on.

In Part Two, so far we have covered the general principles used to evaluate the condition of planets, and an interpretive set of rules to determine their meaning, which we drew from the work of Morin.

Now we need a framework, the general house blueprint that gives you a structure to tie it all together. We will then take a walk around the lot and look at a couple of example houses.

The section begins with a comprehensive, step by step outline that you can walk through to delineate a chart using the principles we covered.

After that will be a series of worked out chart examples using the outline, so that you can see the principles at work, in context. Some of the examples are of famous people, and I will give the chart data for them. Two other examples are clients or acquaintances of mine, and those charts will be presented anonymously, with chart data omitted and some personal details omitted or changed.

Before we cover the chart interpretation outline, there are a couple of important general principles that I suggest you keep in mind at all times.

Evaluate the condition of a planet or point before interpreting

The first step to delineate the meaning of any planet, is to review its essential dignities or debilities. This gives you an idea of the basic condition of the planet.

Always look at rulership and exaltation, detriment and fall. If you want to get further detail you can include the 3 triplicity rulers and the term ruler. I rarely if ever look at the dignity of face, although strictly speaking it is part of the system.

The second step is to review the other, accidental dignities that affect the planet's condition - house position, speed, direction, other planets aspecting it, and so on. This gives you an idea both of the *visibility and power* of its action, and of other ways its action is changed in quality.

Keep the sect of the chart in the background of your mind

A planet's action is strongly colored by whether or not it is in the same sect as the chart. It is not the main factor in the planet's performance, but it should not be forgotten.

Look at the Stakes for any point

Any planet's action will be affected by planets in the same sign, and planets in the signs that oppose or square.

Notice Whole Sign Aspects

In traditional astrology, whole sign aspects are primary, and degree aspects are special case. The whole sign aspects are particularly important for planets in the stakes.

Examine Reception when looking at aspects

When you are examining the interaction between two planets, what kind of aspect they have, or whether they are averse, take time to see if there is any reception between them at any rulership level. Regardless of the planets or aspect, two planets with reception will work out much differently than if there were no reception between them. Reception is a powerful measure of influence and of the ability to work together.

Chapter Twenty Six:
Chart Interpretation Outline

The purpose of this outline is to give you a structured, step by step procedure to follow when interpreting a new chart. It will train you to be able to pick out the important points in the chart that need further focus.

Not all the planets are equally important, and typically there will be one or two that dominate the meaning of the chart. This outline can help you find those important points, and the life areas that they affect.

(Note - Even if you use the 3 modern outer planets, I suggest that you go through this outline first with only the Sacred Seven. That will give you a grounded base of interpretation. You can then go through the outline a second time with the outer planets added, and note what changes.)

* Scan all the planets for their condition.

Start with the the two major dignities, rulership and exaltation, and their debilities, exaltation and fall. Check to see which planets are in particularly good or bad shape.

Note which planets have a major essential dignity or debility. If more than one, check for aspects between them. It is likely that any planets that are in either very good or very bad condition will be important focuses for the native. Also remember that any debilitated planets will not necessarily be negative in outcome, but they will be challenging.

* Look at the angles

Planets on or near the angles, especially the Ascendant and Midheaven, will be strong, visible and important.

You can also check the mode of the Ascendant - cardinal, fixed, mutable - for a general style of acting in the world. If the Midheaven is in the 10th house, it will be in the same mode as the ascendant, which will make that style of acting more important.

When using Whole Sign houses, also look at the tenth house whether the Midheaven is there or not

Check which house the Midheaven is in, as it will likely be important to the native's sense of vocation or calling.

* *Look at sect*

Determine if it is a day or night chart, then check the 2 benefics and the 2 malefics.

Other things being equal, the planets in the sect of the chart will be more helpful or less harmful; the planets out of sect, less helpful and more harmful. Other dignity, house location and aspects can modify this rule.

Note especially the benefic in the chart sect (aka the Good Guy), and the malefic out of sect (aka the Bad Guy). Look at their location, condition, and the houses they rule, for likely sources of benefit or trouble.

* Look at the *Lord of the Ascendant*, and *planets in the first House.*

The first house represents the native, so any planets there will be primary.

* Go through the planets for *balance of modes*
(cardinal/fixed/mutable), and balance of elements (fire/air/water/earth). Notice any distinct emphasis or lack, any imbalance. Mode was weighted more strongly than element balance in traditional texts, and that matches my experience.

* Check for the *closest aspects by degree*. Again, examine the planets by house position, dignity and reception.

By this point in the process there should be one or two features of the chart that stand out. I typically find that a chart revolves around a few important planets or houses. Look at those in more detail. If a major theme has emerged by this point, you can drop the outline and follow the trail.

There is one other point I suggest scanning for as part of this first pass.

* Examine *the planets in the stakes* with any important planets in the chart. All of the planets in that cross-shaped set of houses will tend to be activated at that same time.

Other Patterns to Notice

If you want more detail, here are some other important points that are worth examining.

* **Examine the *Moon and Mercury*** and their relationship and condition.

With the Moon as emotions and Mercury as intellect, the relationship between these two planets shows relationship of thinking and feeling, and which the native values the most. How they aspect, or if they are averse, can show if they are aware of each other.

* **Check the *Lot of Fortune*** - This Lot can often describe where they native's greatest sense of Fortune is, what they value highly, where they would most like to be fortunate or where they place a lot of value. Which house it is in, any planets in the same house, and placement and condition of its lord, say a lot about how the Lot of Fortune is likely to play out.

* **Check the *general distribution of planets***. I am not referring to the classes of chart shapes that Marc Edmund Jones formulated in the early 20th century. Here I refer to just generally where the planets are. Are they mostly above the horizon, or below? Or, are they clustered in a single part of the chart? Are most the of important ones in a couple of houses, and how do those houses aspect?

* **Check for *antiscia and contra-antiscia***. Once you learn the pattern they do not take long to scan for. Since aspects by antiscia use a very tight orb you will not always find a significant connection, but if you do it is worth taking notice.

* **Check for *heliacal rising,*** where a planet is emerging from under the Sun's rays within a week of birth. You need an ephemeris to do this easily. Often such a planet will emerge into prominence in some way.

The inverse of this is ***heliacal setting***, in which the planet is going into the Sun's rays; this can indicate that the planet's effect will be hidden, eclipsed or reduced in some way.

If, by this point, you do not have a good idea of the chart - go back and start again. Once you get a sense of how this process works that will happen very, very rarely.

General Condition (Dignities) to Evaluate

Once you have picked out the main points in the chart, go over the following list of areas carefully. The first scan was for general evaluation. At that point you can go more thoroughly into the important points you picked out in the above process.

This is the same procedure you can use for any area of interest or specific subject area in the chart. If it is a subject, you would start with the house that rules the subject area. If that house contains any planets, start there. If not, look to the ruler of the house.

Check for the following conditions.

- dignities, essential and accidental

- debilities, essential and accidental

- the house the planet is in, and if there are other planets in that house

- the planet ruling the house or point - its placement and condition, and whether it is in aspect or in aversion.

- the houses and planets ruled by them - in aspect or in aversion?

- whole sign aspecting planets in 'the stakes' - conjunction, opposition, square

- closest degree based aspects, applying and separating

- receptions in general - how planets do or do not receive each other

- antiscions and contrantiscions

Interpretation and the Lots

Other than the Part of Fortune, the various Lots are usually looked at when you want to go into a specific subject area in greater detail. They are part of the second phase of chart interpretation, after the initial scan has been completed.

Section Six: Examples of Interpretation

Example One Introduction: Mars Rising

I want to give an example here of interpreting a single important planet by putting together all of the building blocks we have gone over.

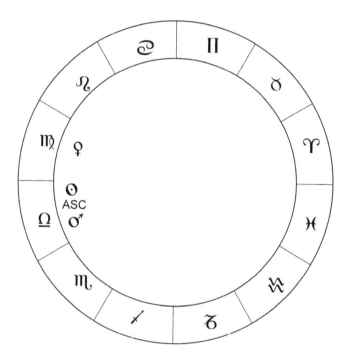

Figure 21: Mars Rising

The example chart shows Mars in Libra, rising in the first house, conjunct the Ascendant. The sign ruler of Libra, Venus, in in Virgo in the twelfth house.

Here is a step by step interpretation of Mars, just using the building blocks.

First of all, Mars will act like Mars regardless of condition.

This is a day chart - the Sun is just above the horizon. Mars is nocturnal, the chart is diurnal, and so Mars is out of sect and a malefic. This planet may be a source of trouble depending on its condition.

Mars is right on the Ascendant, near the strongest angle. So this planet will be very strong and prominent in the native's life, possibly the dominant planet in the chart. Mars is in the first house so it will be a major part of the native's personality.

Mars in in Libra, the sign of his detriment - so, off-balance, not in control, and things will have a tendency to fall apart. Combine this with being out of sect and this planet is likely hard to control and a source of problems. There is an uneasiness, a tension and a restlessness here.

Mars is in Libra, a cardinal air sign - air (warm and moist) is an element that connects, Mars (hot and dry) tends to separate so they work at cross-purposes. The person thinks of themselves as friendly and agreeable (Libra) but doesn't always act that way (Mars). Mars is hot and air is warm so those qualities will reinforce each other.

Air is intellect and communication so those are the likely the areas in which Mars will act.

Libra is cardinal, and Mars acts quickly, so Mars action will be quick and strong, but probably not be sustained. Mars could act as big bursts of enthusiasm for things that then peter out quickly. Or, the native could get impatient easily. Or, the person may want to come across friendly but come on too strong and seem abrasive or pushy. Or, the native may start projects but not follow through (Mars in detriment, things falling apart). Or, when under pressure, Mars could express as irritability or outbursts of anger that pass quickly - probably verbally rather than physically expressed since this is an air sign.

The ruler of Libra, Venus, is in her fall in Virgo, and is in the 12th House, which does not aspect the Ascendant. So the ruler is averse, does not see Mars. This means that how Mars acts is likely out of the awareness and control of the person. However, Mars is right on the Ascendant, so it will be visible to others. The person may not realize how they come across to others.

Mars is conjunct the Sun, in the condition called being combust or burnt. Among other things, planets that are combust are hidden so they are out of awareness. That further emphasizes the effect of Mars ruler being averse. Being conjunct the Sun right on the Ascendant the Mars is a prominent part of the person's personality but is out of awareness, too close to see.

Mars rules the 2nd house of finances, and the 7th house of primary relationships. With Mars being out of sect, malefic, and in bad condition, these two areas that Mars rules are likely the main source of problems in the native's life. It is also likely that those problems arise from impulsive actions by the native which they are not completely aware of and do not feel in control with.

We will now take this interpretation of a meaning of Mars, and place it in the context of the entire chart in the example that follows. I wanted to use this introductory section to point out how very far you can go by just looking carefully at the building blocks for a single planet, and thinking them through.

Example One: Female Native

This chart example is done anonymously, and I have removed the data from the illustration. We will walk through the chart interpretation outline a step at a time, and I think you will see that, by the time you have walked through the steps of the chart interpretation outline, you will have a very good idea of the overall meaning of this chart.

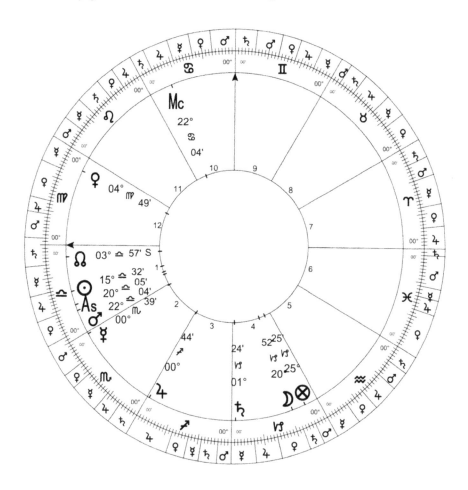

Figure 22: Chart of Female Native

Note: *In the example chart wheels, the outer ring shows the Term rulers for that section. For example, in this chart, Saturn in the 4th house is in the Terms of Mercury.*

Pl	Ruler	Exalt	Tripl	Term	Face	Detri	Fall
☉	♀	♄	♄☿♃	♃	♄	♂	☉ -
☽	♄	♂	♀☽♂ +	♀	☉	☽ -	♃
☿	♂	--	♀♂☽	♂	♂	♀	☽
♀	☿	☿	♀☽♂ +	☿	☉	♃	♀ -
♂	♀	♄ m	♄☿♃	♀	♃	♂ -	☉
♃	♃ +	☋	☉♃♄ +	♃ +	☿	☿	--
♄	♄ +	♂ m	♀☽♂	☿	♃	☽	♃
☊	♀	♄	♄☿♃	♄	☽	♂	☉
⊗	♄	♂	♀☽♂	♄	☉	☽	♃
As	♀	♄	♄☿♃	♃	♃	♂	☉
Mc	☽	♃	♀♂☽	♃	☽	♄	♂
☋	♂	☉	☉♃♄	♃	♂	♀	♄

Table 17: Dignities for Example One

Scan Planets for their condition

Notice in the first house, that the Sun is in fall in Libra, and Mars is in detriment. Both planets are conjunct each other and conjunct the Ascendant. You will see as we go along that this group of three, especially Mars, will serve as the pivot point of the entire reading. With the two problem planets conjunct the ascendant, her life challenges will be of her own making, the result of her own actions.

Venus is in fall in Virgo, and is in the 12th house.

Both Saturn and Jupiter are in their rulership, and the Moon is in its detriment.

So, two of the planets are in rulership, two in detriment, and two in fall; six out of the seven planets have a major dignity or debility. That is very unusual. I would not be surprised if this person's life was a study in emotional extremes.

Look at the Angles

First, the mode - both the Ascendant and the Midheaven are cardinal, so we can expect this person to have a cardinal way of acting in the world - good at starting things, active, maybe impulsive, not always good at follow-through.

As for planets on the angles, the first planet that jumps out is Mars. We noticed earlier that Mars is in detriment, so this is a planet to watch. Notice also that Mars has cardinal kinds of characteristics - impulsive, active, and good at starting things. With Mars in detriment we can deduce that not being good at follow through is also likely. So Mars is strong and visible by angle, but off balance and in detriment by essential dignity.

The other planet near an angle is the Moon, which is in detriment in the fourth house. Notice also, as long we're there, that the Moon is also conjunct the Lot of Fortune. What the Moon represents is probably very highly valued by the person. Being in the fourth house, this probably means family, home, and a rootedness in those things. Being in detriment, she is insecure and shaky there.

With Moon in the 4th in detriment, it is likely that this person will be private about her feelings, not able to express vulnerability easily. It is also likely this person strongly values the security of a family and a home, and wants to feel rooted there, but does not always feel secure.

Look at sect

The Sun is just above the horizon in the first house, so this is a diurnal or day chart.

Both the diurnal benefic Jupiter, and the diurnal malefic Saturn, are in their rulership, so both planets should have a positive effect in her life.

Jupiter is in the 3rd house, and also rules the 6th house. With the 6th house lord in his rulership it is likely the person is physically healthy and able to recover from illness well. (Although we did not discuss it at length, it appears that she has a basically strong and healthy constitution, that most of her illnesses were acute (cardinal, Mars on ASC) rather than chronic, and that she bounces back and recovers.)

Third house would mean good relationships with her siblings, and probably positive experiences in school, and maybe a liking for learning. Jupiter in Sagittarius also has an aspiring and spiritual bent, and is in the

3rd/9th house axis of spirituality, so we can expect that to be an important supportive part of her life. That Jupiter could also be a teacher or role model she looks to for support and meaning, possibly from an alternative spirituality since it is third house rather than ninth.

With Saturn in the 4th house you have a secure support of family, although being Saturn it is likely not very warm or emotionally intimate. Saturn is responsibility rather than fun.

Saturn also rules the 5th house of children, which also could indicate support of children, a sense of loyalty and responsibility towards her children.

Now examine the out of sect planets. Mars, the out of sect malefic, is right there on the Ascendant. *Mars again; this planet is important!* Mars rules the 7th house of relationships and the 2nd house of finances and resources, so it is likely this person's largest areas of challenge are in those two areas. With Mars being in detriment, the problems likely arise from impulsive, thoughtless behavior.

(When I opened the reading for her by mentioning those two areas she basically said something to the effect of, "Exactly right! How did you know that! You have to teach me how you did that!" Those were not her exact words, but the exclamations give an idea of the tone of her response. I'm already feeling some of that impulsive Mars energy jumping up.)

The out of sect benefic is Venus, who is in Virgo in the 12th house. Venus has dignity by triplicity in an earth sign, but a 12th house placement is weak, out of awareness, out of control. We will talk more about Venus in the next point.

Look at the Lord of the Ascendant, and planets in the first house

We already mentioned Mars and the Sun. *Notice Mars is popping up repeatedly as we go through scanning these points.*

Mars in the first house often signifies the kind of childhood in which the person is always running into things, and probably getting her share of head cuts and bumps. This was true.

Venus is the ruler of the Ascendant, weak in the 12th. Also, the ruler of the Ascendant is averse, so there is likely a lack of awareness of how she appears to other people. (Her mom used to tell her, "Honey, you just don't get how you come across.") That Venus in the 12th is not in a position to exercise any rulership control over the first house.

Look at Balance of Modes and Elements

Four out of seven planets are cardinal, two mutable, and one is fixed. Cardinal dominates, and the two angles are also cardinal, so we expect strongly cardinal characteristics to her life.

The elements are a mix - 3 earth, 2 air, 1 fire, 1 water. I did not give this any weight in the reading.

Check for closest aspects by degree.

It starts to get interesting here.

Mars is conjunct the Ascendant by 2 degrees. Mars and the Ascendant are both tightly square the Moon in the fourth house, and Mars is in a position of an overcoming square. *Mars again.*

With Mars tightly square Moon, you have an insecure Moon in the 4th house hidden away, being guarded by a brash impulsive Mars on the Ascendant. I took that to mean that this person, when feeling insecure (moon in detriment), or if her family or security was threatened (moon in 4th), possibly by unstable finances (Mars ruling 2nd), that she would tend to get compulsive, irritable, panicky and maybe hysterical (Mars in detriment) and could react with anger or bouts of shouting, where she was not really aware that she was doing that. (All of that was confirmed.)

Notice also that the Sun, Ascendant and Mars are all conjunct within 7 degrees in the first house. This makes Mars combust. In this case Mars is quite strong, but being combust tends to make it out of her awareness. Notice that the out of awareness theme came up when we saw that Venus, the Lord of the Ascendant, is in the twelfth house, averse the first house and is in her fall. This theme of the native not being aware of how she comes across has appeared repeatedly and is important. *Notice particularly that she is not aware of how that Mars comes across to other people.* Her impulsiveness is largely out of her awareness and control.

Notice also that Mars is conjunct Mercury cross-sign by around 8 degrees, and Mars is ruler of that Mercury in Scorpio. We have a Mars flavored intellect here. Mars is in Libra, an air sign, so it is likely that a lot of her Mars energy gets channeled into mental, verbal, intellectual pursuits. (As I understand it she worked for a newspaper as an investigative reporter.)

Other aspects - Saturn is tightly sextile Mars, so Saturn probably has a stabilizing effect. Saturn is in the 4th house of ancestors, and this woman had a grandmother (older relative, Saturn in 4th) who was a real source of support and a spiritual role model for her. Being sextile it takes work and effort, which are Saturnian things, and likely will get better as she gets older, also Saturnian.

Jupiter is square Venus, and Mercury is sextile Venus. With that Jupiter being in his rulership in the third house, it turns out that this person basically structures her life as her spiritual path (Jupiter), and that she looks to strong teachers as her spiritual role models (also Jupiter). Many of her role models she finds through reading and classes (Jupiter again, and Mercury), and she is drawn to self-sacrificing kinds of paths like Vedanta (12th house Venus, a house of sacrifice or self-undoing. She chooses paths that teach self-undoing.)

What do we do about that Mars?

At this point we figured out that Mars is a dominant planet in her personality, and that her problem areas are the two houses ruled by Mars, the 7th of primary relationships and the second house of finances. She was married for many years, then impulsively left her husband to have another major relationship that ended up being very negative and destructive for her, and that fell apart (ruler of seventh house in detriment). Her finances were unstable throughout her life, and at the time I met her she had left that destructive affair, and was back living with her ex-husband and children, but had little money of her own. Notice that her husband was a source of support as part of that strong fourth house. This is a relationship that both had problems as a marriage but was strong as a family.

I want to look at ways to deal with that Mars, and I want to do that by looking at the planets that have dignity where Mars is located.

Mars is in Libra; the ruler of Libra is Venus, but she is in the 12th house,

in her fall and averse. We can't look for much help, control or support
there. Just wanting to be loving, gracious and Venusian won't do much
good.

Saturn is exalted in Libra, and Saturn is in his rulership in the 4th house,
and aspects the Ascendant. So, Saturn could have a possible good affect
here. Further, notice that Saturn is in Capricorn, and Mars is exalted
there, so these two planets are in each others' exaltation.

We have mutual reception by exaltation here.

We hit the jackpot. That suggests that these two planets should be able to
work together very well indeed. (I mentioned earlier that Saturn seemed
to be related to a grandmother she looked up to - someone she exalted.)

I suggested that having secure family support, and a secure living
situation, was very important to her(Saturn in rulership in 4th), or that
there might be older relatives who were sources of support.

Notice that Saturn in his rulership is in the same house as the Moon in
detriment. On the one hand this would tend to dampen expression of
emotion. On the other hand, it could give her a sense of duty and
responsibility to others, and a structure that could help discipline her
energy. As I mentioned, she had family members who were strong
spiritual and supportive role models, and she used that sense of
responsibility to help stabilize her life.

We look to Saturn to have a positive effect on Mars because Saturn has
strong positive dignity in the house Mars is located, and has good
essential dignity. A planet with dignity has influence and responsibility.
The mutual reception by exaltation means that the interaction of the two
planets is mutually positive.

As it turns out, the triplicity rulers of Libra, an air sign, are Saturn,
Jupiter and Mercury; two of those planets are in rulership, and all three
are woven together to give her spiritual path, her role models, her reading
and writing. Mercury in Scorpio would be good for a reporter, good for
someone who intellectually explores deep spiritual paths.

Also, Mars rules Mercury in Scorpio, so it appears that a lot of her Mars
energy was channeled in Mars Scorpio sorts of ways - a deep, driven sort

of search. Also, she was an impulsive book buyer, and like most people interested in astrology, owned a lot of books (Mercury in the second house of possessions - she valued Mercurial objects, books, on deep subjects, Scorpio.)

The Mars energy expressed in the houses that Mars ruled.

The actions commenced in the house in which the planet resides (impulsive action from the first), and the results were in the subject areas of the houses ruled (seventh house of relationships and second house of finances) The second house has the planet Mercury, which is related to reading, study, writing, investigation.

One other thing I would like to note before we conclude - the two planets associated with the father, Saturn and Sun, are both quite strong in this chart, and the two planets associated with the mother, Moon and Venus, are quite weak. Also, the Sun is conjunct the Ascendant. As it turns out this woman did identify with her father much more than her mother, and he apparently was the dominant personality of the two.

We could go further, but I think you get the idea that walking through the interpretation outline, step by step, and taking the normal meanings of the planets, houses and signs we found, wove a very vivid and distinct picture of this person's life. Fleshed in by feedback from the native we could get very specific, so there was no mind-reading involved here. Notice how the same sorts of themes kept popping up over and over again.

The entire process was just following rules, and trusting that what the chart was saying was true.

Notice also that, although this reading has its share of character analysis - which figures, with the dominant planet being conjunct the Ascendant - *not all of the chart is inside the person's mind.* In this chart especially the strong planets Jupiter and Saturn were other people in her life, her living situation, or her family. *Those planets were not her attitude towards those areas, they were the people and outer circumstances.*

Example Two Introduction: Jupiter Rising

Our second example is of a prominent living person. Before we go on and look at the entire chart, I want to give a quick example of interpretation just using standard meanings of a single prominent planet.

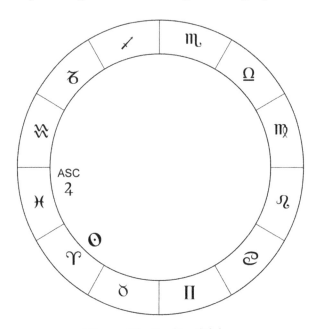

Figure 23: Jupiter Rising

The native has Jupiter rising, tightly conjunct the Ascendant, in Pisces.

Any planet conjunct the Ascendant will tend to dominate the chart, so we should be able to tell a lot about the person from this one planet.

This is a night chart, so Jupiter is not in sect. Jupiter is benefic, so the further dignity of the planet will be important.

Jupiter is in his rulership in Pisces. That makes him very strong, prominent, in control. Jupiter is also in the triplicity and terms of Mars, so there could be a strongly assertive aspect to its action. Combine this with Jupiter being out of sect, and a basically strong and powerful planet may get a bit edgy. However, being in his rulership and a benefic the effect of this planet will be mostly positive and definitely strong.

Jupiter also rules the 10th house of career and reputation. The native is likely to be highly visible and powerful in their chosen career.

Jupiter rules, among other things, law, religion and the church, so the native is possibly a prominent and powerful person in one of those areas. Both Sagittarius and Pisces are mutable signs. Sagittarius, as mutable fire, should have a strong mental component that has to do with philosophy, aspiration, and working with philosophy as ideas that tie things together - maybe a scholar or theologian, a lawyer or college teacher.

Not a bad start to the interpretation of the chart of Joseph Ratzinger, also known as Pope Benedict.

There is another possible way of interpreting Jupiter here as out of sect. Sect has a political connotation, and is connected to the party in power at a given time. Ratzinger is Jupiter in an organization, the Catholic Church, which is out of sect in terms of the modern world. The Church is no longer the ruling power, the prevailing worldview. So, Ratzinger is a representative of an out of fashion, out of authority, out of sect church.

I don't think that particular interpretation of an out of sect planet as connecting the native to an out-of-favor group, is a traditional usage of the term. However, I have found it to be very significant in enough charts to pay attention.

Example 2: Joseph Ratzinger, Pope Benedict XVI

We will walk through the outline a step at a time with this chart, and watch the meaning unfold. This means there will be some repetition from the Jupiter only scan we just finished.

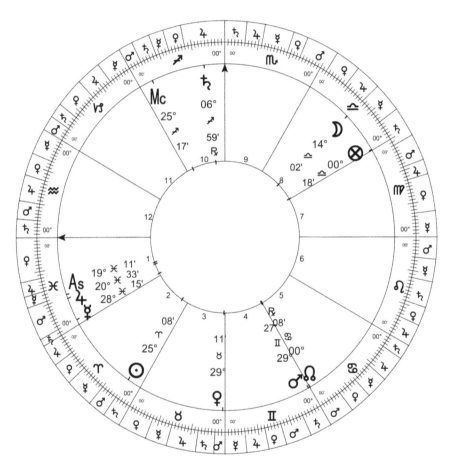

Figure 24: Pope Benedict XVI
April 16, 1927
4:15 AM
Marktl, Germany

Scan the Planets for condition

As we noted, Jupiter is in his rulership, as is Venus in Taurus in the 3rd house. However, Venus is in a very late degree, so there is some instability there.

Pl	Ruler	Exalt	Tripl	Term	Face	Detri	Fall
☉	♂	☉ +	♃☉♄ +	♄	♀	♀	♄
☽	♀	♄	☿♄♃	♃	♄	♂	☉
☿	♃	♀	♂♀☽ m	♄	♂	☿ -	☿ -
♀	♀ +	☽	☽♀♂ +	♂	♄	♂	--
♂	☿	☊	☿♄♃ m	♄	☉	♃	--
♃	♃ +	♀	♂♀☽	♂	♂	☿	☿
♄	♃	☋	♃☉♄ +	♃	☿	☿	--
☊	☽	♃	♂♀☽	♂	♀	♄	♂
⊗	♀	♄	☿♄♃	♄	☽	♂	☉
As	♃	♀	♂♀☽	♂	♃	☿	☿
Mc	♃	☋	♃☉♄	♄	♄	☿	--
☋	♄	♂	☽♀♂	☿	♃	☽	♃

Table 18: Dignities for Pope Benedict

In addition, The Sun is exalted in Aries.

So we have three planets strong with a major dignity.

In addition, Saturn in the tenth house has minor dignity by triplicity.

Interestingly, the one planet with debility is Mercury, which is in its detriment and fall in late Pisces. This is in the chart of an extremely intelligent scholar, teacher and theologian who had an enormous influence on the theology of the Catholic church in the latter half of the 20th century and beginning of the 21st.

This clearly shows that a debility does not mean that a planet's effect will end up being negative. I have often seen that, if there is a single seriously debilitated planet, it can end up being the person's greatest strength, since so much work goes into making it work well. That surely seems to be the case here.

Look at the Angles

We have already noted that Jupiter is right on the Ascendant in his rulership, and I think we demonstrated that planet dominates the chart.

The other angular planet is Mars, who is around 4 degrees from the Nadir or IC in the fourth house. Mars will come up again a little later in our analysis.

Saturn is not angular, but he is in the tenth house of public vocation, in Sagittarius, a sign ruled by Jupiter and associated with religion. If you used a quadrant house system Saturn would be in the 9th house of the church. The association shows up in both house systems.

Saturn in the tenth house often signifies someone who comes to a position of power and influence after much hard work, but then suffers ill fortune and a fall from power. I think we can see that in the sexual scandals that blighted Benedict's term as Pope.

Look at sect

This is a night chart; the Sun is in the second house, below the horizon.

The benefic of the sect is Venus in Taurus, in the third house, which in this case I think stands for personal spirituality and devotion as opposed to the public face of the church in the ninth. I have read some of Ratzinger's writings on Mary, and I think that he has a deeply mystical, personal sense of devotion that he keeps private, that is the foundation of his faith. That fits Venus in Taurus.

The malefic of the sect is Mars, in Gemini, an air sign ruled by Mercury, in the 4th house. Note that Mars is tightly conjunct the North Node, which will tend to magnify this planet. Ratzinger had a reputation of being very orthodox and severe - his nickname was, the "Panzer Cardinal". Mars has dignity by triplicity in the first house where Mercury is, so there what is called a mixed mutual reception between the two planets. I've read some of Ratzinger's interviews, and I think that Mercury/Mars blend comes across when he is fighting for the church and purity of doctrine.

The benefic out of sect is Jupiter on the Ascendant, and the malefic out of sect is Saturn in the 10th. Saturn rules the 11th house of friends, and the 12th house of hidden enemies. It appears that Ratzinger, while very powerful, was not particularly popular, and I would be very surprised if he did not have adversaries working against him in the convoluted politics of the Vatican.

So Jupiter's dominance is very strong, but not very relaxed or benevolent. This man was very influential, but viewed himself as fighting against the tide of a modern society that would dilute or undermine the faith he was fighting to defend.

There is another interesting relationship by reception. The moon is in Libra in the eighth house, which is averse the ascendant. This is fitting for a man who seemed to keep his personal emotional life severely private. The moon is ruled by Venus, who is in the exaltation of the Moon in Taurus, with Venus dominant since she is in her rulership. There is a mixed mutual reception between Venus and the Moon. I am surmising that the one outlet for his emotions was in his personal devotion; other than that they were likely kept severely out of consciousness.

I think that Venus and the Moon reflect the private inner life of Ratzinger, while Jupiter dominates the other planets and shows his public face.

Look at the lord of the Ascendant and planets in the first house

Jupiter is both lord of the first house and is in the first house. Mercury is also in the first house, loosely conjunct Jupiter by around 8 degrees. I think that conjunction with Jupiter is part of what made Mercury turn out so strongly. Mercury is always strongly colored by whatever planet most closely aspects it. (We will see a close Mercury/Mars aspect a little further on.)

Looking at the terms of the planets here is interesting. Recall that, when we discussed the terms, that it is a low-level dignity that has to do with how the planet is finally earthed or manifest. Saturn is in the the domicile and terms of Jupiter; Jupiter is in the terms and triplicity of Mars, Mars is in the terms of Saturn and the triplicity of Saturn, Jupiter and Mercury; and Mercury is in the terms of Saturn. So there seems to be a tightly knit intertwining of these planets that colored this man's strong and severe intellect, all under the dominance of that Jupiter.

Check for balance of modes

Both angles are in mutable signs, as are four of the seven planets. mutable is associated with matters of the mind, and Ratzinger was basically a theologian, writer and teacher.

Check closest aspects by degree

Jupiter tightly conjunct the Ascendant dominates.

Mercury is also in a tight applying square with Mars, with Mercury dominating. That fits the combative intellect.

Check the stakes of the dominant planets

Jupiter dominates, and the planets in the stakes with Jupiter are Mercury, Saturn, and Mars. We already talked about how tightly intertwined those planets are.

We could go further, but I think that we have laid out the main themes in the chart. All we did was follow the rules and go with the standard meanings.

Example 3: Female Native Two

This is the chart of an acquaintance and client of mine.

In this example, we will pursue important points in the outline as they emerge. That is typical; working through the outline highlights an area of attention, so you focus on that area and explore it.

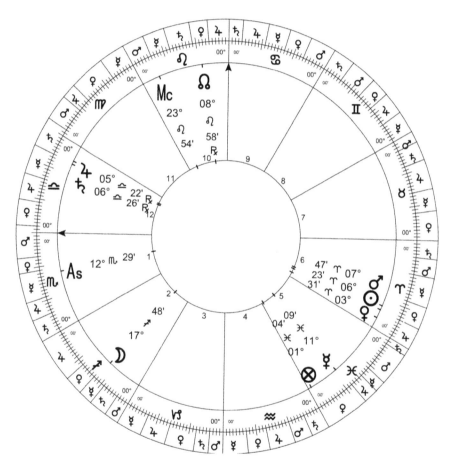

Figure 25: Female Native 2

Scan Planets for Condition

The Sun is exalted in Aries, Mars is in rulership in Aries, and the two planets are tightly conjunct. We know right away that these two, and whatever patterns they are in, will likely be the focus of the chart.

Venus is in her detriment in the same sign, conjunct the same two planets.

Both Jupiter and Saturn have dignity by triplicity in Libra, and Saturn is also exalted in Libra. In addition, Saturn is in his joy in the twelfth house. Values like duty, responsibility and self-sacrifice, which are both Saturnian and twelfth house, are very strong for the native. She exalts those values.

Pl	Ruler	Exalt	Tripl	Term	Face	Detri	Fall
☉	♂	☉ +	♃☉♄ +	♀	♂	♀	♄
☽	♃	☋	♃☉♄	☿	☽ +	☿	--
☿	♃	♀	♂♀☽	♀	♃	☿ -	☿ -
♀	♂	☉	♃☉♄	♃	♂	♀ -	♄
♂	♂ +	☉	♃☉♄	♀	♂ +	♀	♄
♃	♀	♄	☿♄♃ +	♄	☽	♂	☉
♄	♀	♄ +	☿♄♃ +	☿	☽	♂	☉
☊	☉	--	♃☉♄	♀	♄	♄	--
⊗	♃	♀	♂♀☽	♀	♄	☿	☿
As	♂	--	♂♀☽	☿	☉	♀	☽
Mc	☉	--	♃☉♄	☿	♂	♄	--
☋	♄	--	☿♄♃	♀	♀	☉	--

Table 19: Dignities for Female Native Two

Mercury is in detriment and fall in Pisces in the 5th. Mercury is close to the Lot of Fortune.

Look at the Angles

Notice that there are not any planets within 15 degrees of the angles either way. So, no planets are very angular and visible.

It is also worth noting that four of the seven planets, including Mars and Sun which we noticed before, are all cadent, in the sixth and twelfth houses.

At this point, since that important set of planets in the sixth and twelfth houses has come to our attention, it is worth pausing from the outline to examine them in more detail.

This person will not be famous or prominent in any way. With that many planets in cadent houses the native will likely be involved in an occupation that is unglamorous, behind the scenes, with no authority.

The sixth and twelfth houses are associated with illness and health care, and people with their dominant planets in these houses are often concerned in this area.

The native is a nurse, and her main work is in extended care facilities (twelfth house), in which the patients are confined to the facility. You do not get any more unglamorous, hard working, no authority job than nurse in an extended care facility.

The twelfth house has to do with hospitals and places of confinement, and she works mainly with the aged. Saturn rules old age and death, and recall that Saturn is in his Joy in the twelfth house; he belongs there. The native has taken Saturn in the twelfth house and turned it into her vocation.

The mode of both angles is fixed. It is likely the person will be persevering, maintaining, probably stubborn, a good person to have on your side for the long haul. This is very true, and was manifest when she put herself through nursing school over a four year span while working part time. Once she decides to do something, she stays with it, period.

Look at sect

This is a night chart; the Sun is in the 6th house, below the horizon.

The two nocturnal planets, Mars and Venus, are both conjunct the Sun in the sixth house. Mars is very strong, Venus is in detriment and combust, in tight conjunction with the Sun. Mars is also conjunct, but in his rulership, so there are no ill effects on Mars from being combust.

The native is hard working, stubborn, determined, and does what she sets her mind to. With Mars that strong she can also have a temper, and the one time she became seriously ill was an incident in which she became very, very angry but did nothing to express it - that is Mars strong in the sixth house. She was bedridden for a few days but recovered soon, which would reflect Mars being strong in the sixth house. Her illnesses are mostly acute and brief, and she recovers quickly.

Mars and Sun in a cardinal sign are both very energetic but need time to recharge after a burst of energy. This condition conflicts with the fixed angles, and the native can push herself to the point of exhaustion and illness because she doesn't take breaks. Over the years she has figured out that this does not work.

Mars is definitely representative of many of her strongest characteristics.

Regarding Venus in detriment, the native dresses plainly and does not wear makeup, and does not overly groom her appearance. While attractive, she is not particularly feminine in demeanor and style.

When we look at the out of sect planets, another clear pattern emerges. Both Jupiter and Saturn are in the twelfth house of confinement, bad fortune, and obscurity; both are retrograde; they are conjunct; and, looking ahead, they are both in tight opposition to the Sun/Mars/Venus grouping.

Both Saturn and Jupiter can be associated with the father; in the twelfth house they can be a missing father. The native's parents were separated when she was two years old, and she was raised in a single parent household by her mother.

Venus in detriment is significant here. Venus can represent her mother, in detriment because a single parent - in a weak position, off-balance. Venus is conjunct the Sun, and the native strongly identifies with her mother. Her mother's life was dominated with raising her throughout her childhood, which also matches the symbolism of the Sun/native completely swallowing up and dominating Venus/her mother's life.

An aspect of opposition, with the symbolism of the number 2, can often mean a relationship, and the native did and does maintain an ongoing relationship with her father even though he is missing from the household.

Saturn, the out of sect malefic, rules the third and fourth houses of family and siblings. That can reflect the challenge of the separated parents, and being raised in a single family household.

One final note; I have seen that people with strong sixth and twelfth houses are often driven by a strong sense of duty and self-sacrifice. That strongly applies to the native here. That strong sense of duty is also related to Saturn here.

With family stability having been her main source of challenge growing up that, combined with her sense of duty makes her fiercely loyal to her mother and to family in general. She will sacrifice anything for family.

Balance of Modes

We have already noted the two angles in fixed signs.

Looking at the modes, five of the seven planets, that group involved in the 6th/12th house opposition, are all in cardinal signs. So, along with the fixed angles giving her a strong, stubborn, loyal streak, this native is very cardinal in that she is independent minded, and acts on her own. That also fits the symbolism of Sun/Mars in Aries. With all the pressure of that cardinal opposition with the fixed angles, there is a certain driven quality to the native. She is always active, always busy, and she does not relax easily.

Looking at the elements, six of the seven planets are in fire and air, and there are no planets in earth. Fire and air are the active, outgoing elements, and water and earth the passive and receptive elements; we already noted the native is always busy and active (fire), and constantly is with people and can talk a blue streak (air), but has a hard time laying back and relaxing (water). Lack of earth could indicate a lack of stability, but that is somewhat compensated by the angles being in fixed signs.

Closest aspects by Degree

We have already noted the 3 planets conjunct in the sixth house tightly opposed the 2 planets conjunct in the twelfth house. It is clear by now, that one tight opposition pattern defines the main themes of her life.

Or, rather, most of them.

Mercury in Pisces is in detriment and fall in the fifth house of children. Notice that the Lot of Fortune is also in the fifth house. We mentioned the part of fortune as indicating where the person's happiness or heart is, and the native has always been sure she wanted children. However, with that 6th/12th duty axis, work came first, and she did not have her first child until age 29.

The native is now in her mid 30's and has two young children. As you can imagine, it is a lot of work for her to balance work as a nurse with caring for children that young, but as you would expect, she is stubborn, determined, dedicated, and very hard working with a strong sense of service. And, she seems to be happiest when she is spending time with the children. Her heart, her Fortune, is there.

Interpreting the Lots

This is a good place to look at a couple of the additional Lots, to give an idea of how they add some psychological depth to the chart.

We already noted that the Lot of Fortune is at 1 degree Pisces in the fifth house. In a night chart, Fortune is the Lot of the Moon, since that is the point the calculation of the Lot begins. The *Lot of Venus* is tightly conjunct, at 2 degrees Pisces. The connection of Venus and the Moon with motherhood and love underlines how important children are to her.

The *Lot of Children*, which falls at 9 Scorpio, conjunct her Ascendant by around 3 degrees, in the first house. The first house is identity, ruled by the dignified Mars in the 6th. She identifies with her children; they are part of her primary identity, and a very high value for her. She has the same sense of obligation, service and total caring towards her children that she takes towards her work.

Also important in this chart is the *Lot of Friends*, which falls in Leo in the 10th house, nearly conjunct the Midheaven, in the same house as the North Node. The Lot is ruled by the Sun which is exalted in the 6th and conjunct her Mars. She values her friends very highly; I think it fair to say that she 'exalts' them, like her Sun. Having that Lot right on the MC, in the same house as the North Node, and ruled by an exalted Sun, will all tend to underline the importance of her circle of friends in her life.

I think those two lots are particularly important, since there is nowhere else in the chart that shows how important her children and friends are to her. The Lots gives us a window into her inner life, her values.

And finally, the *Lot of Work* is in the twelfth House - we already talked about her vocation as nurse serving in extended care facility. This just underlines the importance of her work to her, and that she has found her correct vocation.

Switching the chart to Placidus house System

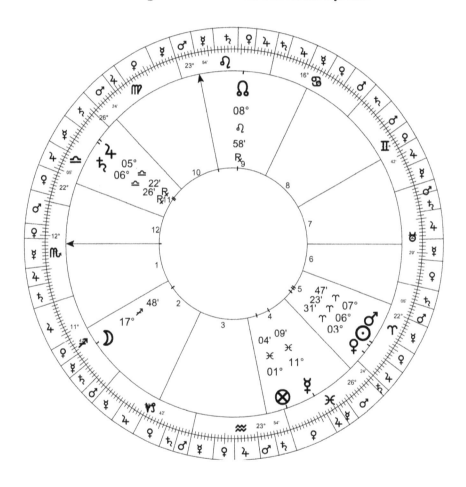

Figure 26: Female Native, Placidus Houses

I want to give an example here of how looking at the chart with a different house system can provide different information. In this chart, as in all the examples, we have been using Whole Sign houses. I now want to look at the same chart using the Placidus quadrant house system.

Notice that the 5 planet opposition, with Sun, Mars and Venus at one end in Aries, and Jupiter and Saturn at the other end in Libra, now falls across the fifth and eleventh house axis.

With 3 planets in the fifth house we would expect that children would play an important part in this person's life, and with two planets in the eleventh house we would expect that friends are also very important, and that she is loyal to her friends in the way she is loyal to her nursing work. This happens to be true for the native, and both are very important parts of her life, as mentioned previously.

In this house system, Saturn, which we have seen can signify the father, is in the eleventh house of friends. In this axis, the relationship with her father could include time with groups of friends, and with fifth house creative activities.

Notice that the 6th/12th house emphasis in the Whole Sign house system is important, but the 5th/11th house emphasis in Placidus is also important. In this particular case, both house systems were needed to do justice to these parts of the native's life.

This alternate house view sheds light on the meaning of another one of the Lots.

The *Lot of the Father* falls at 12 Taurus, in the seventh house, tightly conjunct the Descendant and opposite the Ascendant. We have taken Saturn as standing for the father, in opposition aspect to the native. Here, the Lot is in opposition to the Ascendant, which parallels that aspect. Recall that the opposition, based on the number 2, also stands for relationship, and this Lot points out that the native's relationship to her father has been more like a one to one equal relationship, since the father was not the primary caretaker. This complements the opposition in the 5th/11th axis as it appears in Placidus. We have already noted that the opposition can be an aspect of relationship.

Example 4: Carl Jung

Our next example is that of the famous psychologist Carl Jung.

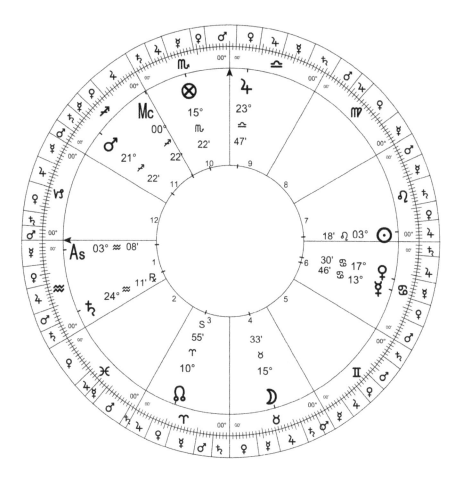

Figure 27: Carl Jung
July 26,1875
7:32 PM
Kesswil, Switzerland

Planet Condition

Saturn is in his rulership in Aquarius in the first house, and is also the only planet in the first. The ruler of the first house being in the first house makes this planet very strong and distinct.

Pl	Ruler	Exalt	Tripl	Term	Face	Detri	Fall
☉	☉ +	--	♃☉♄ +	♃	♄	♄	--
☽	♀ m	☽ +	☽♀♂ +	♃	☽ +	♂	--
☿	☽	♃	♂♀☽	☿ +	☿ +	♄	♂
♀	☽ m	♃	♂♀☽ +	☿	☿	♄	♂
♂	♃	☋	♃☉♄	♄ m	♄	☿	--
♃	♀	♄	☿♄♃ +	♀	♃ +	♂	☉
♄	♄ +	--	☿♄♃ +	♂ m	☽	☉	--
☊	♂	☉	♃☉♄	♀	☉	♀	♄
⊗	♂	☉	♃☉♄	♂	♀	♀	♄
As	♄	--	☿♄♃	☿	♀	☉	--
Mc	♃	☋	♃☉♄	♃	☿	☿	--
☋	♀	♄	☿♄♃	☿	♄	♂	☉

Table 20: Dignities for Carl Jung

The Sun is in his rulership in Leo in seventh house, and is very strong being right on the Descendant.

The Moon is Exalted in Taurus, and there is Moon in Taurus to Venus Cancer mutual reception! Both of these planets are also quite strong.

If you look at the chain of rulership in the chart, the Moon and Venus together rule most of the chart. So, in this chart the Moon dominates Mercury.

The Moon is the night, the unconscious, the realm of dreams and emotions.

Four out of the seven planets in Jung's chart are very dignified, and none are debilitated. That is quite unusual.

Angles

The Sun is dead on conjunct the Descendant and thus very strong. There is a very nice symbolism to the Sun in Jung's chart being right on the borderland between day and night, realm of the Sun and realm of the Moon, conscious and unconscious. The Sun is just setting, about to commence his journey through the underworld.

Saturn is in the first house about 20 degrees in, which is definitely angular, and we already noted Saturn is in rulership.

Those two planets should have a dominant influence in Jung's activity in the world.

Concerning the Sun in the seventh house as partnerships, Jung was very fortunate in his marriage, and had a very loyal, wealthy and long-suffering wife. Also, his work in psychotherapy involved intense one-on-one relationships, focused on the other person. In therapy the other person shines and is visible, and Jung the analyst is safely hidden with Saturn in the first house. Saturn in Aquarius is also the Wise Old Man archetype and the teacher of ancient wisdom. The common image of the older Jung looking serious with his pipe fits this archetype.

Sect

The Sun is right on the Descendant, so this birth took place at sunset. That close to the horizon the light of the Sun was probably still visible, so I would opt for this chart being diurnal or day.

Out of sect Planets

Mars is peregrine in Sagittarius in the eleventh house, and rules the third and tenth houses. We should expect that problems with profession/reputation, and family, siblings and schooling should be areas of challenge. Finding a community to fit was also a likely challenge. There is another possible effect of the peregrine, wandering Mars - Jung apparently slept around a lot and had numerous affairs, including with students (Mars ruling the third house) and professional colleagues (Mars ruling tenth house) and that did cause stresses and problems.

Venus, is in the sixth house of slaves and employees, conjunct mercury. He was very fortunate to have intelligent women workers/slaves/disciples that were under him, sometimes in more sense than one.

Venus is a stronger planet than Mercury in Jung's chart, and his thought was permeated by a Venus sort of perception of pattern, proportion, analogy, metaphor, and meaning. Synchronicity is a Venus kind of concept; it views patterns as a whole and in context.

In sect Planets

Saturn is in rulership in the first house but is retrograde, and Saturn rules both the twelfth and first houses. There is a connection between his sense of self and an extreme sense of privacy or hidden secrets, which fits the connotation of both Saturn and the twelfth house, where Saturn has his joy. Saturn also rules stone, and Jung worked in stone throughout his life, including building much of his house from stone.

Jupiter has dignity by triplicity in Libra in the ninth house of philosophy, religion and dreams, and Jupiter is ruled by Venus. Jupiter rules both the second and eleventh houses. Jung was fortunate in finances, both from his marriage and from higher education, philosophy and travel. Also, his groups of friends (eleventh house) grew out of his work in the ninth house area of dreams and philosophy.

Lord of ASC & planets in first

Saturn is lord of the first and is in first house, which gives Jung his serious, saturnine, wise man persona that he presents to the world. You have the stereotype photo of Jung looking wise and gnomic with his pipe. Saturn also rules old things, and ancient wisdom, and is associated with recovering old things or studying old subjects, and as we noted, Saturn also rules the twelfth house of secrets. All of this relates well to Jung's long, slow tedious (Saturn) research work uncovering the meaning of alchemy and gnostic texts, and then writing about them very ponderously and seriously. This saturnine quality is also expressed in his personal secretiveness.

Modes and Balance

The Ascendant is fixed, with two planets very strong on the ASC/DSC axis the fixed quality is strongly accentuated. The Midheaven is mutable - his reputation had to do with his philosophy and his introspective ideas and interests, which fits mutable.

Closest Aspects by Degree

We already mentioned the Sun conjunct the Descendant being related to his wife, and to his profession which depended on intense one on one encounters focused on the other, the patient.

Saturn is trine Jupiter very tightly, with Jupiter overcoming as the dominant planet. His sense of self, and his purpose, is ruled by ninth house concerns including dreams, academia, and philosophy. His writing being academically reputable was very important to him - he wrote to appease that Jupiter.

Jupiter in the ninth house could also refer to the dream authority figures he dialogued with in his own internal work that was recorded in the posthumously published Liber Novus, also known as the Red Book.

There is good reception here between Jupiter and Saturn. Jupiter is received into Saturn's exaltation, and Saturn is received into Jupiter's triplicity. This reception and aspect makes that Jupiter that much more important and influential, and enhances the coordination of the two planets.

Jupiter also gets good reception from Venus in good condition in mutual reception with Moon and conjunct Mercury.

The Moon is sextile the Mercury/Venus midpoint, within two degrees of sextile to both planets, with the Moon the earlier and the overcoming planet. The Moon in the fourth house at the bottom of the chart could be the inner world of dreams, and of a connection the past. With the Moon and Venus being very strong Jung had a strongly emphasized inner feminine side. He exalts the realm of the Moon, the realm of dreams, of the past.

The Moon rules Mercury, and Mercury here has dignity only by term. I would interpret this as meaning Mercury is dominated by that Moon and by the Venus conjunction. That Mercury/Venus link could also be the aesthetic side of Jung - his paintings, his Red Book. Jung's thought was not rational and detached, it was aesthetic, imaginal, emotional, Moon/Venus flavored.

The most elevated planet is Jupiter in the ninth house of philosophy, religion, dreams and oracles. The ninth house is ruled by Venus which is conjunct Mercury, so Jung's dream life and religious life were expressed in creative artistry and through his writing.

Personality

Mercury and Moon are sextile, with the Moon earlier stronger, stronger and dominant. This is related to his inner private sensitive self, the attention he paid to emotions, to dreams and images, and to the inner life in general.

Mercury and Saturn, ruler of the first house, are averse. Saturn dominated his writing and communication style, but you often get the sense that he is trying to hide as much as reveal. Much of his writing is ponderous, footnote-laden, but also vague, implying, suggestive.

The world saw Jung as Jupiter in the tenth house, the Teacher, and Saturn in the first house, the Old Wise Man. The strong angular planets are the ones that are most visible and active in the world.

Example 5: Timothy Leary

If you were even vaguely conscious any time around the mid 1960's to mid 70's you were aware of Timothy Leary, who was either a freedom fighter or an evil drug fiend out to destroy our nation's youth, depending on your perspective.

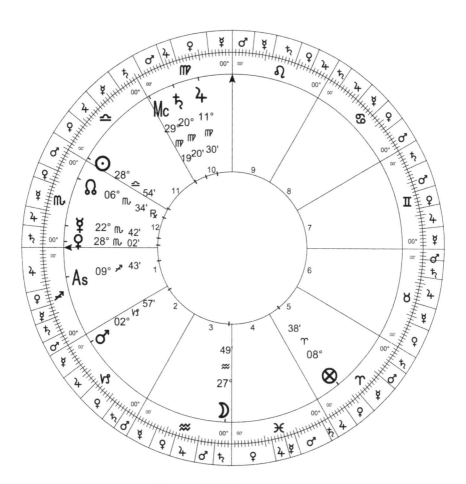

Figure 28: Timothy Leary
December 23, 1958
12:00 PM
Santa Monica, California

Tim Leary was best known for popularizing LSD and advocating its use as a psychological tool for healing and evolution of consciousness. He was arrested in the 70's for drug possession and made a very famous and daring prison break, was eventually found and re-captured.

			Essential Dignities				
Pl	Ruler	Exalt	Tripl	Term	Face	Detri	Fall
☉	♀	♄	♄☿♃	♂	♃ +	♂	☉ -
☽	♄	--	♄☿♃	♄	☽ +	☉	--
☿	♂	--	♀♂☽	♃	♀	♀	☽
♀	♂	--	♀♂☽ +	♄	♀ +	♀ -	☽
♂	♄	♂ +	♀☽♂ +	☿	♃	☽	♃
♃	☿	☿	♀☽♂	♀	♀	♃ -	♀
♄	☿	☿	♀☽♂	♃	☿	♃	♀
☊	♂	--	♀♂☽	♂	♂	♀	☽
⊗	♂	☉	☉♃♄	♀	♂	♀	♄
As	♃	☋	☉♃♄	♃	☿	☿	--
Mc	☿	☿	♀☽♂	♄	☿	♃	♀
☋	♀	☽	♀☽♂	♀	☿	♂	--

Table 21: Dignities for Timothy Leary

After his release from prison he spent the remainder of his years as a writer and public speaker advocating freedom of consciousness.

I chose this chart for an example because of ways that the literal meanings of some houses and planets were played out in the most famous events of his life.

Planetary Condition - Dignity/Debility

The one planet with major dignity is Mars exalted in Capricorn in the second house, his rising planet. Leary at his prime was physically strong, quite handsome, and charismatic.

Jupiter is in detriment in the tenth house of career and reputation, which is ruled by Mercury. A planet in detriment does not function well, or starts well and then falls apart.

Jupiter in the tenth house could also be his short-lived Castalia foundation, which he founded as a place to explore the potential of LSD.

The Sun is in fall in the eleventh house of friends and groups. Planets in fall feel like they are not taken seriously, not listened to, disrespected, so they can crave attention, or act in ways to pull the spotlight onto them. The Sun rules the 9th house of higher education, philosophy and travel, which is where Leary wished to shine, and early in his career he was a well known and brilliant professor at Harvard.

Venus is in detriment in Scorpio in the twelfth house conjunct his Mercury. Taking standard meanings, this is self-undoing (twelfth house) through 'undignified' Venusian pleasurable activities related to Mercury, the mind. The twelfth house also signifies prison.

Mercury in the twelfth house of self-undoing is his writing and ideas that led to his downfall, arrest and disgrace.

Note that Mercury rules the tenth house of public office - Leary was tracked down and arrested shortly after he ran for public office; he was a candidate for governor of California. So the tenth and twelfth houses, connected by Mercury's rulership, were linked in that specific circumstance.

The twelfth house is also hidden enemies, or enemies working covertly, behind the scenes for his downfall.

The meaning of those twelfth house planets is frighteningly literal and very apt.

We have two planets in detriment, one in fall, and only one, Mars, in positive dignity. Planets in detriment promise a lot but don't deliver, or start well but then have things fall apart.

Angles

Jupiter and Saturn are both in the tenth house, but prior to the Midheaven by several degrees, so they are cadent by strength. In a quadrant house chart, those two planets would be in the ninth house of academia, religion, philosophy, dreams. Also, Jupiter followed by Saturn in the tenth house could also be rise to fame and fall from grace.

Sect- the chart is diurnal with the Sun in Libra in the eleventh house.

The main planets in sect are Jupiter in detriment, and Saturn peregrine in the tenth house, ruled by Mercury in the twelfth house, and we already mentioned prison related to his public persona and reputation. Other than being in sect these two planets are in poor shape, and they are highly visible in the tenth house.

Looking at the planets out of sect, Mars is exalted in Capricorn is in the second house and is the rising planet, and Mars rules the twelfth & fifth houses. This creates another connection between pleasure (5th) and prison (12th), and Mars out of sect can be rebellious activity.

The other out of sect planet is Venus in detriment the twelfth house, and we already looked at the connection of Venusian activities and self-undoing. I have sometimes found that the phrase 'undignified Venus' can be taken in the ordinary connotation of the word undignified.

Lord of Ascendant & Planets in First

Jupiter rules the first house from the tenth, is peregrine, and is ruled by Mercury. With Jupiter in the tenth house I get the feeling he loved being in the limelight, which would also be related to his Sun being in fall .

Sagittarius rising can also be "foot in mouth disease", someone who speaks his mind regardless of consequences, or doesn't realize the implications of what he says. It can be an optimistic and highly idealistic sign, but not always well grounded.

Distribution of Planets

Both the tenth and twelfth houses have two planets each, and we have noted the numerous ways the two intertwine. I think that those two houses and their interaction dominate the chart and his life.

Modes, Angles and Balance

The angles are both mutable, hence intellectual and mental.

There are four planets mutable, two cardinal, and one fixed, so mutable dominates. We have seen this repeatedly in charts of people who are distinguished primarily by their ideas, their mental activity. In Leary's case even the subject of his thinking and writing was consciousness itself.

I think we can stop at this point, since the major features of the chart keep coming up over and over.

Example 6: Friedrich Nietzsche

In this final chart interpretation I will give an example of how to appropriately include the modern outer planets in the interpretation. In this case there are some strong and tight aspects to outer planets that add significantly to the meaning of the chart.

I also wish to demonstrate that the meaning of a chart can apply on every possible level. Along with details of his life, this interpretation should give a window into the nature of his thinking, writing and philosophy.

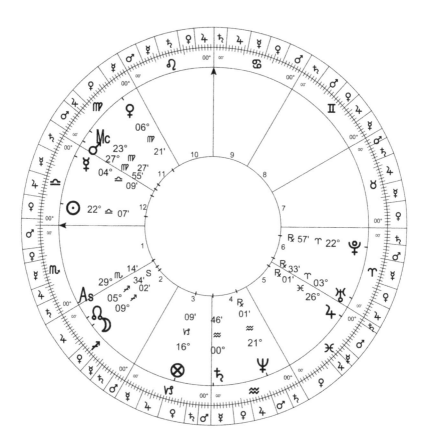

Figure 29: Friedrich Nietzsche
October 15, 1844
10:00 AM
Rocken, Germany

Pl	Ruler	Exalt	Tripl	Term	Face	Detri	Fall
☉	♀	♄	♄☿♃	♀	♃	♂	☉ -
☽	♃	☋	☉♃♄	♃	☿ m	☿	--
☿	♀ m	♄	♄☿♃ +	♄ m	☽ m	♂	☉
♀	☿ m	☿	♀☽♂ +	☿	☉	♃	♀ -
♂	☿	☿	♀☽♂ +	♂ +	☿	♃	♀
♃	♃ +	♀	♀♂☽	♂	♂	☿	☿
♄	♄ +	--	♄☿♃ +	☿ m	♀	☉	--
☊	♃	☋	☉♃♄	♃	☿	☿	--
⊗	♄	♂	♀☽♂	♀	♂	☽	♃
As	♂	--	♀♂☽	♄	♀	♀	☽
Mc	☿	☿	♀☽♂	♂	☿	♃	♀
☋	☿	☊	♄☿♃	♃	♃	♃	--

Table 22: Dignities for Friedrich Nietzsche

Scan Planets for Condition

Saturn is in his rulership in Aquarius in the 4th house, but is cadent because he is a large distance after the angle. Being in the fourth house I suspect this applies to his father, who was a minister and died while Nietzsche was young. Also, Nietzsche was raised in a strict idealistic atmosphere.

Jupiter is in rulership, in Pisces in the fifth house, conjunct the angle of the IC and the bottom of the chart, so Jupiter is very strong. I associate this planet with his extreme philosophic creativity, the exuberant idealism that was in some sense quite philosophically religious. He believed in the goodness of philosophy and that was his religion, the faith, on which he built his life. We will see later that this planet plays a very mixed role in this chart, sometimes adversarial, sometimes inspirational.

There is one other planet that has major dignity that is not obvious at first glance. If you look carefully at Mars in Virgo, it has dignity by triplicity, and also by term. Having two minor dignities was considered equivalent to having one of the two major dignities, so we count Mars as one of the dignified planets.

Venus and Mercury are in mutual reception, Virgo to Libra, and Nietzsche was considered a beautiful writer and stylist.

The Sun is in Libra in fall in the twelfth house. We mentioned that a planet in fall feels like it isn't heard. This matches the extreme sense of isolation and loneliness that he had, and exactly like fall, the sense that no-one respected him or listened to him. That matches both a planet in fall and a planet in the twelfth house, so it is doubly accented.

The twelfth is also a house of extreme self-sacrifice and of self-undoing, which I think matches Nietzsche's attitude, that he was sacrificing all he had in the name of the Truth, and of the new, possible human he sometimes called the Ubermensch or Overman.

The Sun in the twelfth house rules the tenth house of reputation, so his career, profession, visibility, reputation were all ruled by obscurity, oblivion, lack of respect and self-sacrifice.

Look at Angles

The North Node, about 8 degrees after the Ascendant, is conjunct the Moon which is the rising planet about 10 degrees after the ascendant. The Moon is in Sagittarius ruled by Jupiter, conjunct the North Node, which is also Jupiterian, amplifies and magnifies, giving a kind of extreme aspiring emotional idealism. For all his criticism of the all-too-human, there a sense he is an extreme idealist with a very high vision of what the human should become. That sounds like Moon in Sagittarius, an aspiring moon which is magnified by the Node.

Near the Midheaven is Mars, 4 degrees away, and Mercury is about another 7 degrees after. Mars and Mercury together set much of the tone for that belligerent, sharp, attacking intellect.

Notice that those four points, Mercury, Mars, the Midheaven and Venus are all lined up within 30 degrees, with the Sun just 18 degrees after. Mix equal parts Mercury and Venus, beautiful, elegant writing and perceptive intellect and wit, and tie in that belligerent, attacking, critically aggressive Mars and that Sun in oblivion, and I think you've got a pretty good description of Nietzsche's style.

Note that Mars rules both the Ascendant and the sixth house of illness. Nietzsche was plagued by vicious migraine headaches for most of his life - Aries is associated with the head - and mental illness claimed him in 1899, 11 years before his death. Also note that Mercury in the twelfth house rules Gemini, and the eighth house of death, representing the mental illness that claimed him.

Jupiter is in conjunction to the IC by around a 2 degree orb, in that fifth house which can be linked to creativity. That Jupiter is also in tight opposition to Mars in picky, critical Virgo. I get a sense of an extreme idealism and non-orthodox sense of - not spirituality, but what I'd want to call the spirit or heart of the man - he believed deeply in the Universe, and in what the human could become (Jupiter), but that was in some ways undercut or opposed by his severe, even Spartan sense of intellectual honesty (Mars) - he would tolerate no weakness or spiritual fuzziness in anyone including himself. You repeatedly see a sharp dichotomy between a Spartan, self-denying discipline and a heart yearning to believe.

Sect

This is a diurnal chart. The two big day planets, Saturn and Jupiter are both in their rulership and so are strong, positive and influential. We already touched briefly on Jupiter. As we mentioned previously, solid Saturn there in Aquarius in the 4th is probably related to his father the minister as a severe, demanding and grim role model, as being at the base of Nietzsche's own attitude and values. Actually I suspect that the father's influence is present in both Jupiter and Saturn.

Looking at the out of sect planets, there is Mars conjunct the Midheaven which we already mentioned, and also Venus in the same sign, and both Venus and Mars are ruled by Mercury in the twelfth house. I have sometimes seen that, when important planets are out of sect, that it can mean that the native experiences being out of touch with the times, out of power, out of style. Being out of sect means that the planets would act in ways that were edgy, uncomfortable, sometimes off balance, and not at ease or at home. That surely is the case here.

Lord of Ascendant

Mars again. That belligerent, out of sect, warrior Mars seems to be the dominant planet in the chart as far as Nietzsche's personality, his face to the world, went. Attacking single-handedly anything he viewed as false or dishonest or outdated - it was a vicious, attacking off-balance Mars with an out of sect kind of attitude.

We have an important point here - Mars is lord of the Ascendant, and is conjunct the Midheaven. That makes this planet the most visible, the most defining in terms of how he appears to the world, and it is the planet that he identified with. It also means that his work, his destiny, and his identity, are one and the same. Nietzsche lived for his work, and had a strong sense of mission. Mars and the Midheaven in the eleventh house by Whole Sign can mean that much of his purpose is related to finding kindred spirits, the community he belongs with, those who share his values and vision. It also means that Nietzsche will play a challenging, adversarial Mars role in his communities.

So Mars is in a mutable sign, picky, critical Virgo, ruled by a twelfth house Mercury, and the ruler of Mars is averse; it is likely that how this Mars came across was somewhat out of Nietzsche's awareness. I think it very likely that he really didn't realize how shrill and attacking his writings could be. Mars is ruled by that twelfth house Mercury, where the more he screamed, the less he felt like anyone was listening at all.

Remembering that Mars is out of sect, and we should expect it to act off balance in some ways, edgy and belligerent. Nietzsche was known for advocating the Will to Power, and favored a morality of the strong and aggressive. Mars is in a mutable sign ruled by Mercury, and all of Nietzsche's aggression was channeled into words, intellectual attack.

Here is a quote from an introduction to Beyond Good and Evil (section 259), describing Nietzsche's concept of the ethics of the noble or master class. The tone of the out of sect Mars comes through very clearly.

> "The higher civilizations, we read, arise when men with natural instincts, barbarians in every sense of the word, men of prey possessing unbridled strength of will and an unquenchable thirst for power, throw themselves on weaker, more peaceful races...For life is essentially appropriation,

*injury, conquest, suppression, severity; exploitation does
not belong to the depraved but to the very nature of life, life
as a manifestation of the will to power." (p.xix)*

That key concept, Will to Power, is determined and colored throughout
by the dominant Mars.

Note that that Mars, right on the Midheaven, is the most elevated planet,
the highest, and represents what he most highly elevated, his supreme
value. With Mars in a critical mutable sign, his supreme value was an
intensely honest and brave mind.

Balance of Modes

The Ascendant is fixed but the Midheaven is mutable. In addition, 4 of
the 7 planets are mutable and 2 cardinal, so there is a predominance of
mutable. As we have repeatedly noted, mutable is often associated with
intellectual and introspective energies; not an actor but a thinker.

Closest Aspects by Degree

Mars is conjunct the Midheaven, Jupiter is conjunct the Nadir or IC, and
Jupiter is in tight opposition to Mars. I think that opposition is the axis
that rules the entire chart, and it expressed in many ways. We have the
tension between his high idealism and his extreme critical side. From
another angle, we could read Jupiter as standing for the faith of
Christianity, and Mars is the rebel, the Antichrist.

Looking at the reception between Mars and Jupiter, Mars has dignity by
triplicity in Pisces, but Jupiter is in detriment in Virgo. Jupiter's reception
towards Mars is positive, Mars' reception towards Jupiter is negative.
This would accentuate the adversarial nature of the opposition, which
strengthens the symbolism of Jupiter as Christianity, which Mars rebels
against.

Saturn is trine Mercury by 3 degrees, which could give his intellect a
naturally severe and structured side. I think that also speaks of the
influence of his father on how he worked philosophy.

Venus is square Moon by 3 degrees, I think there is a tension between
Venus and the Moon along similar lines to the tension between Mars and
Jupiter, that stress of the high idealism and extreme criticality.

Outer Planets

I think we are making very good sense out of Nietzsche's chart with just the traditional seven planets. However, in this case, I do want to look at the three outer planets, as there are significant degree aspects that greatly add to the interpretation.

We already mentioned the strong Mars/Mercury opposition. When you add in the outer planets, there are two other very strong opposition aspects, and they are in the same area of the chart.

Uranus is tightly opposite Mercury. This gives an intellect that is constantly high strung, stimulated, brilliant, rebellious, shooting off sparks. There is surely a Promethean and Uranian quality to Nietzsche's stance. The Uranus opposition is from the sixth house of illness, and I think that ties in well with his constant ill health, his headaches and mental stress, and his eventual mental collapse.

The Sun is tightly opposite Pluto. This is the man who wrote that Man is something that must be overcome, and taught a philosophy of constant self-transformation.

Those two oppositions strike me as VERY important! Add those to our interpretation and you get someone who is tense, high strung, constantly pressured - there is no relaxation in this chart, everything is at a fever pitch.

This chart is dominated by three strong opposition aspects, and his philosophy was polarized in opposition to what he viewed as a decadent, unhealthy older religion and culture. Nietzsche was defined by opposition, what he stood against.

The Stakes with Important Planets

We already mention the Midheaven axis, which includes Jupiter, Mars, and Venus. In the stakes with those planets there is also the Moon on the North Node. That's a pretty intense batch of planets.

Mercury and Moon

These two planets are sextile by sign but not a very tight orb, around 5 degrees. In this case I would say that the extreme idealism is at the service of that piercing intellect, and that the two were intertwined.

One other miscellaneous note - Mercury is approaching the Sun, eighteen degrees away and closing - so he is going through a heliacal setting. Mercury in the twelfth is being gradually eclipsed and burned up. (A modern astrologer might look at secondary progressions to see what age Mercury became burnt up by the Sun.)

Antiscia

There is a tight antiscia connection in this chart, between Mercury and Jupiter, and that relation acts like a shadow or background conjunction. That surely fits a philosopher! Notice, though, that the Jupiter 'shadow' is not immediately visible, just as it is not immediately apparent how idealistic, optimistic and high-spirited (sounds better than spiritual) Nietzsche was behind the attacking belligerence.

If the birth time I have is accurate, which is questionable, then Saturn and the Ascendant are also tightly antiscia connected. That does fit the sense of Nietzsche as being dominated by the shadow of his dead father, and all that his father stood for.

The Lots

I think that some of the Lots will shed further light on Nietzsche's life and values.

The *Lot of the Father* is at 7 Pisces, ruled by Jupiter in the same house. We previously associated the father with Saturn, and her I think we can see that the Jupiter, idealistic side of Nietzsche's philosophy is also associated with his father.

I'm speculating here, but I wonder if that Jupiter in the 5th opposite his Mars is also the voice of Zarathustra in his most famous work. Nietzsche wrote *Also Sprach Zarathustra* in a fit of high inspiration, very close to what might be called taking dictation or being channeled. That Jupiter/Mars and Uranus/Mercury pair of oppositions right next to each other could express in such extreme fits of channeled, inspired philosophic creativity, and Nietzsche/Zarathustra did play a Promethean/Uranian role of destroying idols and announcing the new ideal. This may also be associated with the antiscia connection between Mercury and Jupiter - there is a sense that Zarathustra is Nietzsche's shadow self.

With strong oppositions like the Mars/Jupiter paralleling Mercury/Uranus, one side of the opposition could be experienced as coming from outside of oneself, and I wonder if that is how Nietzsche experienced the Jupiter and Uranus voice of Zarathustra. That could explain the sense of mission, the sense of calling. For the man who is well known for proclaiming that God is dead, he is fanatically driven by something inside of him that was sacred and claimed his total devotion.

So that complex, strong Jupiter could be both the father and church he rebelled against, and also Zarathustra and all that the new ideal stood for.

The *Lot of Work* is at 23 Scorpio in the first house, loosely conjunct the Ascendant, ruled by our friend Mars on the Midheaven. The first house is identity, and Nietzsche identified with his work, his vocation; he said that he often felt he had an important mission to perform. We also had previously noted that the Ascendant ruler, Mars, is conjunct the Midheaven, so this underlines its importance.

Section Seven: Concluding Material

Combining Traditional and Modern Astrology

Now that we have finished our introductory survey of the basics of traditional natal astrology, I want to address the issue of the relation between traditional and modern astrology.

I ask that all you Purists please either put the book down at this point, or leave the room for a few moments while I address the other readers.

To address this point, I want to talk about my journey through different ways of doing astrology, because I think it parallels some of where astrology may fruitfully go in the future.

Modern or psychological astrology was born partly as a reaction against an older, fate-based approach in which the planets and stars are forces outside of us, and astrology tells of us of the events that happen to us largely outside of our control.

That view has its limitations.

In modern psychological astrology all of the features of the chart are inside the individual, and the purpose of astrology is to analyze the different parts of the psyche. You try to maximize your strengths and minimize your weaknesses.

In the latter part of the 20th century this merged with a largely New Thought approach that talks of viewing everything in the chart as positive, and that you can make of your life whatever you will, with enough effort and positive thinking.

That view also has its limitations.

When I was first drawn to traditional astrology several years ago, it was because I was increasingly disappointed with what I saw as the shallowness and vagueness of much of modern astrology. I felt that it left out a lot of dimensions of life, especially where things happen to us outside of our control.

So, I immersed myself in the practice of just traditional astrology for around three years. I eliminated the modern outer planets and asteroids, went back to Whole Sign houses, and worked at interpreting charts in terms of external events and actual outer circumstances. In this system the chart is not inside of me. Rather, it is a map of the world I inhabit, and much of the chart describes external circumstances and events in my life.

That greatly enriched and deepened my practice of astrology. However, I feel like I am now starting to bump up against the limitations of that approach.

A study group I am in recently did a reading for a person who had a really difficult chart, and had dealt with a lot of really hard and abusive situations affecting her and her family. The reading picked up on that. However, this person had grown greatly through the experience, and had a certain solid centeredness and inner strength.

Psychological growth had happened, but I could see nothing in the traditional techniques that let me see that growth. We change through the years in response to life events, and I needed to include techniques that focused on inner growth and evolution.

So, along with profections and primary directions, which are primarily event techniques, I needed to add in secondary progressions, which seem to focus on inner growth.

So, now I am back to including modern astrology techniques in my work. I have added back the outer planets, and while I do not emphasize them as strongly as most modern astrologers seem to, I do find that they can add an important dimension of meaning to a chart interpretation.

I still use the core traditional techniques described in this book, and they serve as the skeleton or basic structure of the chart. I start with them and return to them to keep a sense of proportion.

However, I now do psychological and character analysis astrology also. From working with traditional astrology for years, my approach to psychological astrology has changed and deepened.

Yes, the chart describes something inside of me, but it is not just inside of me. Along with describing external events, there is a sense in which we are open to a larger psychic reality within us. Even describing my 'inner' order, it is a larger order that I am part of, rather than an order that I contain. There is an outsideness even to my insideness.

I think that is where traditional and modern approaches to astrology can fruitfully converge. Push the psychological approach far enough and you get to a point where outside and inside converge. I view a larger order that I am part of and participate in. External events and internal movement in my consciousness are equally part of that order. In that approach, the chart is not inside me, I am inside the chart.

In traditional astrology the planets started out as gods external to us. In modern astrology they became 'just' psychological forces. Now, for me, the planets are again gods, forces larger than me and outside of my control that manifest both within me and outside of me.

For me, traditional and modern approaches to astrology are not opposed. They are different approaches to a larger order that includes both dimensions. Astrology has gotten much larger, weirder and more wonderful.

I hope this book has given you some fruitful ideas and techniques for you to use in your ongoing exploration and study of astrology of any kind, whether purely traditional, modern, or some mix of the two.

I wish you the blessings of the Gods on your journey. May your ongoing relationship with them be deep, meaningful and fruitful.

Suggested Reading
An Annotated Bibliography

Modern Astrology Textbooks

These are my favorite books on modern astrology, and they work well with traditional astrology.

Costello, Priscilla, *The Weiser Concise Guide to Practical Astrology*. Red Wheel Weiser, 2008.

> *This is a good short book to start with if you are new to astrology.*

Tompkins, Sue, *The Contemporary Astrologer's Handbook: An In-Depth Guide to Interpreting Your Horoscope*. Flare Publications, 2006.

> *The best single comprehensive textbook on modern astrology I am aware of.*

Geisler, Pat, *The Plain Vanilla Astrologer*. ACS, 2013.

> *Not a pure beginner's book, but easy to read, with a wisdom coming from long experience, and rooted in practical details.*

Burk, Kevin, *Astrology: Understanding the Birth Chart*. Llewellyn, 2001.

> *Kevin draws on the work of J Lee Lehmann, which uses the five levels of essential dignity. It is an excellent book, but it is worth being aware that Kevin is mixing principles from traditional and modern astrology without noting which is which.*

The Necessary Books on Traditional Astrology

Morin, Jean Baptiste, *Astrologia Gallica Book Twenty One: The Morinus System of Horoscope Interpretation*. Translated by Richard S. Baldwin. American Federation of Astrologers, 1974

> *If you only buy one book on traditional astrology this is it. A*

clear, lucid and practical guide. It is not a beginner's book, but it is approachable.

Brittain, Patti Tobin, **Planetary Powers: The Morin Method**. American Federation of Astrologers, 2010.

This is a workbook with illustrations to teach the Morin method of interpretation outlined in the previous book. This book is not straight traditional astrology. It includes the modern outer planets, and some of the examples use analogy by house, assuming the modern equation of sign and house meanings. If you keep that in mind this book can be very helpful; it is well laid out and clearly explained.

Lilly, William, **Christian Astrology Books 1 and 2**. Astrology Classics, 2004.

_____, **Christian Astrology Book 3**. Astrology Classics, 2004.

This three volume work is the single most famous and important work on astrology in the English language. Book 1 is fundamentals, and Book 2 is the most famous book on horary astrology ever written. The third volume on natal astrology is not as well known and is underestimated. My original ideas for this book you are reading started years ago with Lilly, Book 3.

Dykes, Benjamin, **Traditional Astrology for Today: An Introduction.** Cazimi Press, 2011.

_____, translator, **Bonatti's 146 Considerations**. Cazimi Press, 2010.

Dr. Benjamin Dykes, Ph.D., is the premier translator and scholar in the area of Medieval astrology. He has translated many volumes of original source works from Latin and Arabic. These two books are a good place start to approach his work.

Avelar, Helena and Ribeiro, Luis, **On the Heavenly Spheres: A Treatise on Traditional Astrology**. American Federation of Astrologers, 2010.

An excellent and comprehensive textbook of the elements of traditional astrology from the era of William Lilly, and well worth having.

Houlding, Deborah, **The Houses: Temples of the Sky**. The Wessex Astrologer, 2006.

This is one of my favorite astrology books. It is the best book available on the houses, and I consider this book essential.

Contemporary Books on Traditional Astrology

Crane, Joseph, **A Practical Guide to Traditional Astrology**. ARHAT, 2007.

_____, **Astrological Roots: The Hellenistic Legacy**. The Wessex Astrologer, 2007.

Dunn, Barbara, **Horary Astrology Re-Examined: The Possibility or Impossibility of the Matter Propounded**. The Wessex Astrologer, 2009.

Lehman, Dr. J. Lee, Ph.D., **The Martial Art of Horary Astrology**. Whitford, 2002.

George, Demetra, **Astrology and the Authentic Self; Integrating Traditional and Modern Astrology to Uncover the Essence of the Birth Chart**. Ibis Press, 2008.

This is an excellent blend of solid traditional techniques with elements of modern astrology by one of the finest teachers in astrology today.

Books on Specific Topics

Greenbaum, Dorian Gieseler, **Temperament: Astrology's Forgotten Key**. The Wessex Astrologer, 2005.

Zoller, Robert, **The Lost Key to Prediction: The Arabic Parts in Astrology**. Inner Traditions International, 1980.

Weber, Lind, *The Arabian Parts Decoded*. American Federation of
Astrologers, 1997.

Hill, Judith, *The Part of Fortune in Astrology*. Stellium Press, 2010.

Original Source Material

Dykes, Benjamin, translator. *Introductions to Traditional Astrology:
Abu Ma'shar & al-Qabisi*. Cazimi Press, 2010.

> *After his little introductory book, Traditional Astrology for Today,
> this book is the necessary foundation to approach and understand
> the other translations that Ben Dykes has done. This book also has
> an extensive list of traditional lots.*

_____, *Works of Sahl & Masha'Allah*. Cazimi Press,
2008.

_____, *Persian Nativities Volume 1: Masha'allah &
Abu'Ali*. Cazimi Press, 2009.

_____, *Persian Nativities Volume II: 'Umar Al-Tabari
& Abu Bakr*. Cazimi Press, 2010.

_____, *Persian Nativities III: On Solar Revolutions*.
Cazimi Press, 2010.

Al-Biruni, *The Book of Instruction in the Elements of the Art of
Astrology, Translated by R. Ramsay Wright*. Astrology Classics,
2006.

> *This book has an extensive list of traditional lots plus many other
> lists and tables of all sorts of correspondences.*

Dorotheus of Sidon, *Carmen Astrologicum*, translated by David Pingree.
Astrology Classics, 2005.

Ptolemy, Claudius, *Tetrabiblos*, translated by J M Ashmand. Astrology
Classics, 2002.

Online Resources

http://studentofastrology.com . This is my astrology website. There are resources and handouts here from a study group on traditional astrology that I led for around two years, and which I still participate in as co-facilitator.

http://www.bendykes.com/ . The website of Dr. Benjamin Dykes, Ph.D., authority on medieval astrology and leading translator of traditional texts from Latin and Arabic. Along with his books of translations, Ben has some excellent audio learning resources which are highly recommended.

http://www.chrisbrennanastrologer.com/ . The website of Chris Brennan, a leading Hellenistic astrologer who has some very fine online courses.

http://www.demetra-george.com/ . The website of Demetra George, one of the finest teachers of traditional astrology. She has also done extensive work on the asteroids. The site has a wealth of good learning resources. Very highly recommended.

http://www.renaissanceastrology.com/ . The website of Christopher Warnock, Esq., a practitioner of Renaissance era traditional astrology in the style of William Lilly and other writers of the period. Warnock has several classes on Renaissance era astrology and magic of various types.

Glossary and Index

This is a list of the main astrological concepts and keywords used in the book, with a brief definition and, when applicable, a page reference where it is covered.

Accidental Dignity - Contrast with Essential Dignity. The Essential Dignity of a planet is determined by its Zodiac position and degree. Accidental Dignity is determined by other circumstances or accidents - house location, speed, direction, and aspects to other planets. Essential Dignity shows quality of action, Accidental affects how it manifests. See Evaluation Rules p. 153.

Angle - refers to the two main axes of the chart, the Ascendant / Descendant axis, and the Midheaven / Immum Coeli axis.

Angular - referring to a planet that is near or on one of the 4 angles of the chart. angular planets are considered to be strong and visible in their action. See Modes and Angularity, p. 72.

Applying - an aspect that is getting closer and approaching exactness. See Aspects, p. 118.

Arabic Part - a calculated point that describes a relation between three other points. Also known in Hellenistic astrology as a Lot, q.v. See p. 136.

Ascendant - The point on the ecliptic that is on the horizon at the time of birth. The Ascendant determines the first house in Whole Sign house system, and is the cusp of the first house in quadrant house systems.

Aspect - The word aspect has two different meanings in traditional astrology. As with modern astrology, an aspect is a set of defined angular relationships between planets or points. In traditional astrology, for one planet to Aspect another means that the planets are in each other's line of vision. Planets that do not aspect each other are considered to be averse, q.v. See Aspects on p. 118.

Averse - Planets that are not in a whole sign aspect are said to be averse, meaning they are out of touch, turned away, or out of the line of vision. For instance, a planet in Pisces is averse a planet in Libra. Since planets that are averse cannot see each other, they communicate by reciting rhymed poetry; hence the name.

Benefic - *(a.k.a. Jolly Good Chap!)* A planet that has an effect that is generally moderate, harmonious, pleasant, growth and life promoting. Jupiter and Venus are the two benefic planets. See p. 52.

Besieged - A planet that is separating from an aspect from a malefic, and applying to an aspect to another malefic. The planet is hemmed in, surrounded by difficult aspects coming and going. Between a rock and a hard place; going from worse to worser. See Evaluation Rules p. 153.

Bound - a minor dignity, also called Term. See the chapter on Essential Dignities, page 58.

Cadent - literally, falling away. A cadent planet is in the area just past an angle of the chart going clockwise. The action of cadent planets is weak, not easily visible, and can often manifest as internal processing rather than external action. See Modes and Angularity, page 72.

Cardinal - a bright red bird that resides in the signs Aries, Cancer, Libra and Capricorn, depending on the time of year. See the Modes of the planets, p. 72.

Cazimi - at the heart of the Sun. A planet within 17 minutes from conjunction to the Sun. While a planet that is combust or very near the Sun is burnt up and weakened, a planet this closely exact is considered to be greatly strengthened. It is as if the planet resides at the very heart of the King. See Evaluation Rules, page 153.

Combust - literally, burnt. Refers to a planet conjunct the Sun within 8 degrees. A combust planet is burnt up, fried. You can't see it since it is completely hidden by the Sun's rays, and it loses all its independent strength. See Evaluation Rules, page 153.

Common - another term for mutable. See the Modes, page 72.

Debilitated - A planet having one of the negative dignities, detriment or fall. A debilitated planet is hindered or corrupted in its expression. A planet can also be debilitated or harmed by aspect, or by house, or some other condition in the chart.

Decanate - 10 degree division of the signs. Not the same as the minor dignity called face, which also divides the signs into 10 degree segments. The planetary assignments are derived differently. What most modern astrologers call the Decanates is a system that was derived from Vedic astrology.

Descendant - the point where the ecliptic crosses the horizon in the West. It is opposite the Ascendant.

Dignity - a term referring to a planet's strength or weakness in a particular location. Essential Dignity (see page 58) refers to the rulership it has in any of 5 levels at a given point. Accidental Dignity (see page 153) refers to how its position and aspects in the specific chart strengthen or weaken it.

Diurnal - the daytime. A chart is diurnal if the Sun is above the horizon. See Sect, page 55.

Double Bodied - another term for mutable. See the Modes of the Signs, page 72.

Face - the weakest of the minor Essential Dignities.

Fixed - the signs Taurus, Leo, Scorpio and Aquarius. All the rest are broken. See the Modes of the Planets, page 72.

Heliacal Rising or Setting - A planet that is emerging out from under the Sun's rays - that is, moving to more than 15 degrees away from the Sun - within about 10 days after the native's birth is said to be making a Heliacal Rising. The planet is showing up again after being hidden, and this puts a special emphasis on the planet, as if it is saying, Hi, Notice Me, I'm back! The Heliacal Setting is the opposite, where a planet is getting closer to the Sun, moving from being visible, to moving under the Sun's rays. This de-emphasizes the planet, making it less visible.

Immum Coeli, or IC - the phrase means, the bottom of the heavens. It is the angle of the chart opposite the Midheaven. It is also sometimes called the Nadir.

Lot - a symbolic point formed by a relation between three other points in the chart, See the chapter on the Lots. See page 136.

Malefic - *(a.k.a. Nasty Bastard)* - a planet whose effect is extreme, disruptive, catabolic, destructive, unpleasant. Saturn is called the Greater malefic, and Mars the Lesser malefic. *(The malefic which is out of sect is referred to in traditional texts as the MML, short for Magnus Malus Lupus, or Big Bad Wolf.)* See page 52

Midheaven or MC - the point where the ecliptic crosses the Prime Meridian, which is the Great Circle in the North-South axis from the point of view of the native. The Midheaven is the highest point that the Sun reaches in its apparent daily motion around the earth.

Movable - another name for cardinal - see the section on the Modes, page 72.

Mutable - what you do to it when it won't shut up. Also refers to the signs Gemini, Virgo, Sagittarius, and Pisces. See the Modes of the Planets, page 72.

Nadir - The point in the chart opposite the Midheaven, also called the IC or Immum Coeli, the low point of the heavens.

Nocturnal - pertaining to the night. See Sect, page 55.

Partile - an aspect that is exact in the same numbered degree.

Peregrine - the word means wanderer, and it refers to a planet that does not have any essential dignity at its location. The planet is homeless, rootless, and relies on the dignity of the lord of the sign it is in to determine how well it functions. See Dignity, page 58.

Perfect - An aspect is said to perfect when the planet's degrees meet exactly.

Pluto - a famous Walt Disney animated character. See page 245.

Ptolemaic Aspect - The traditionally used aspects, the sextile, square or quartile, trine, and opposition. They are referred to by Ptolemy in his book Tetrabiblos.

Rulership - the most important of the major Essential Dignities; see page 58.

Sect - referring to the division into day and night, diurnal and nocturnal. Charts are diurnal or nocturnal sect depending on the position of the Sun above or below the horizon, and the planets are divided up into diurnal and nocturnal also.

Separate - when two planets are in aspect that is becoming less exact, they are said to be separating.

Stakes - from any given point, the 4 signs that are at 90 degree angles to that location. See the Geometry of Aspects, page 32.

Succedent - refers to angularity or relation to the angles. A succedent house is one away from the angular house, and is strong, but not as strong as the angle.

Term - a minor dignity, also called Bound. See the Essential Dignities, page 58.

Trigon - a synonym for triplicity, q.v.

Triplicity - one of the minor Essential Dignities (page 58). Each element has 3 triplicity lords.

Under the Beams - a planet that is conjunct the Sun between 8 and 15 degrees. At this point the planet is no longer visible, being hidden by the Sun's rays, but it is not yet close enough to the Sun to be completely burnt up. It is considered to be a debility. See Evaluation Rules, page 153.

About the Author

Charlie Obert has been a student of astrology since before the turn of the century (the year 2000, not the year 1900). Along with a background in modern astrology, he has concentrated on the study of traditional astrology for the past five years.

Charlie is a member of both the American Federation of Astrologers (AFA) and the National Council for Geocosmic Research (NCGR).

Besides traditional astrology, Charlie is particularly interested in Uranian astrology, midpoint and dial work, and is a member of the NCGR Uranian Astrology Special Interest Group. Recently his main focus is on how traditional and modern astrology can learn from and complement each other.

Charlie is a philosophy major, so the different worldviews and values behind astrology systems are a major area of interest. He is also a student of the Tarot, I Ching and other divinatory systems.

For two years, Charlie led a traditional astrology study group in Minneapolis, MN, which included the fine traditional astrologers Ben Dykes and Estelle Daniels as members. The group has recently started up again, and he stays involved as a co-facilitator.

He is also a student of Chris Brennan's Hellenistic Astrology course.

Along with doing astrology consultation in Minneapolis and elsewhere, Charlie is a trainer by vocation, enjoys leading astrology workshops and seminars, and he currently guides students through the Level 1 and 2 NCGR examinations. He is an NCGR certified Level 2 astrologer, and is currently working on his own Level 3 certification.

Charlie can be reached through his website,
http://www.studentofastrology.com,
or at the email address,
charlie@studentofastrology.com.